"...Pastor David Gudgel has put together in this book one of the most creative, enjoyable, and meaningful approaches that I have seen for understanding what the Bible means by what it says. A trip...through the process will not only be informative and instructive, but it will be fun."

Earl D. Radmacher, President
Western Conservative Baptist Seminary

Are you looking for help in understanding and enjoying the Bible? Then you've come to the right place. Written like a car operator's manual, the **Owner's Guide to Using Your Bible** provides practical methods for digging into God's Word. David Gudgel writes in a clear, simple style that will stimulate your desire to study and apply the Bible. He begins with showing you how to find things in your Bible and helps you progress step by step to word, character, and passage studies. Among the study helps included here are "Tune-up" exercises, methods for determining what the Bible means, and study questions. **The Owner's Guide to Using Your Bible** is a valuable guidebook for individuals or groups.

Owners Guide to Using Your Bible

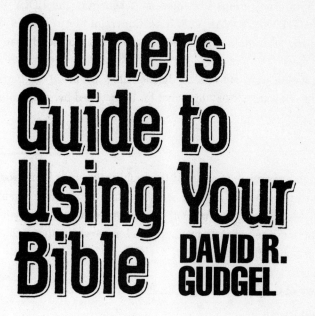

Owners Guide to Using Your Bible

DAVID R. GUDGEL

Power Books

Fleming H. Revell Company
Old Tappan, New Jersey

Library of Congress Cataloging-in-Publication Data

Gudgel, David R.
  Owner's guide to using your Bible.

  Bibliography: p.
  1. Bible—Introductions.   I. Title.
BS475.2.G75   1987   220.6′1   87-12166
ISBN 0-8007-5252-X

Copyright © 1987 by David R. Gudgel
Published by the Fleming H. Revell Company
Old Tappan, New Jersey 07675
Printed in the United States of America

CONTENTS

5

INTRODUCTION

Recently my wife and I purchased a new car. It actually is a used station wagon, but it's new to us. It has plenty of room for the children, groceries, and dog . . . four doors . . . bench seats . . . power everything. We really like our car!

Like most cars, our Ford Fairmont came equipped with an owner's guide. I found it tucked away in the glove compartment. The introduction of this booklet says,

> This Owner's Guide has been written to help you enjoy many miles of motoring pleasure in your new car . . . Your Ford and Lincoln/Mercury dealers want you

to be completely satisfied with your new car. . . .

While no guide can anticipate every possible use, it should be read from cover to cover carefully and kept handy for ready reference. Review the guide carefully and become familiar with all instruments and controls.

This Guide is intended to be a permanent part of your vehicle. Keep it in the vehicle as a ready reference for anyone who may drive it. . . .

By following the various recommendations throughout the Guide and always handling the vehicle in a safe and prudent manner, you can help to assure yourself of enjoyable, trouble-free, and economical pleasure.

Sounds pretty good to me. Who wouldn't want to get enjoyment and complete satisfaction from his new car? I want that. The guide can't give it to me, but it can give me the information I need so my family and I can enjoy our new car's full benefits.

This book has been written with a similar purpose in mind. My intention is to give you a guide that will help you experience the benefits of God's Word in your life. Maybe you are a new Christian and are ready to purchase your first Bible. Or you may have been a Christian for many years but have spent very little time studying the Bible for yourself. Or perhaps you are a Christian who has studied the Word but have found it difficult to understand or enjoy.

This guide is intended to give you information that will help you in five ways: 1. It will help you find your way through the Bible. How is it arranged? Is it written like a novel? Is it written chronologically? Where do the prophets fit? 2. It will help you understand the Bible. Throughout each chapter you will find "Tune-ups." Take some time to do each one. They will help you understand the meaning of God's Word. 3. It will help you apply the Bible to your life. You will find that the Tune-ups are adjusted to help you do this. A Tune-up well done will ensure fewer breakdowns and frustrating experiences in your walk with God. 4. It will give you the answers to the Tune-ups, so you can immediately see that you understand the lesson. These answers are found in chapter ten, "Specifications." 5. It will give you several maintenance schedules to help you in the days, weeks, and years ahead as you study and enjoy your Bible.

Owners Guide to Using Your Bible

ONE

YOUR PURCHASED CAR

Prior to purchasing our car, I decided to look for one that had at least three things: 1. An affordable price. It had to be within a certain price range, and it had to be a good deal. 2. Accessories. Living in Southern California, I wanted air conditioning. I am also a cassette-tape addict, so we wanted a tape player as well. 3. Reliability. I would like to keep it running forever! Low mileage helps here.

Purchasing your Bible was the first step toward successfully studying the Word. Three things set this Book apart from all others.

COMMUNICATION

The Bible you purchased is a unique book: It is the vehicle God has selected for communicating directly with you. In fact, it's God's hotline to you (See 1 Corinthians 2:13; 2 Peter 1:21).

Think of it this way: God is on one end of the line, and you are on the other end. The connection between you has been made possible through the Bible. Through it, He wants to speak directly with you. He wants you to know how to put your life together and how to please Him. He wants you to hear that He loves you and cares for you. He wants you to be intimately acquainted with Him.

Without God's Word, you would be cut off from Him, trying to make sense out of a senseless life. Like King Solomon, your life would be one big frustration. The book of Ecclesiastes describes Solomon's attempt to make sense out of life without God's Word. He uncovered every stone he could find, but he always came away empty. Finally, at the end of his journey, he wrote in Ecclesiastes 12:13: "The conclusion, when all has been heard, is: fear God and keep His commandments, because this applies to every person." Through firsthand experience, Solomon found that life without God's Word is empty, with no rhyme or reason.

You and I are fortunate. We have the privilege of being on the phone with God daily, listening to Him communicate with us through His Word.

AUTHORITY

Your Bible has been stamped authoritatively by God. It stands alone in that it is the final Word as to how one ought to live. Written by more than forty authors from three different continents over a period of more than sixteen hundred years, all sixty-six books are a unified testimony to the divine authority of inspiration from God. God explicitly says in 2 Timothy 3:16, "All Scripture is inspired by God and profitable for teaching, for reproof, for correction, for training in righteousness." Unlike a novel, which may be the personal dream of its own inspired writer, the Bible is inspired by God. All of it is the product of His breath. Although it was written by human authors, 2 Peter 1:21 tells us these men were "moved by the Holy Spirit" to write down the Scriptures, and they "spoke from God." Though these men had free exercise of their natural abilities, emotions, thoughts, and vocabularies, whatever they wrote was authoritative and infallible because of this divine control.

This means the Bible isn't an optional book. You can't take it or leave it as you choose. It requires your utmost attention and diligent obedience. Today only a few share this perspective on the Word of God. In a recent Gallup poll where 1,382 people were asked what book had most influenced their lives, *only 15* cited the Bible. That's hardly more than 1 percent!

The final issue in respect to your Bible is whether or not you see it as the authoritative Word of God. If it is, then you must accept it. If you reject it, then you are in the troubled waters of humanistic reasoning.

"The Bible," D. L. Moody said, "is the traveler's map, the soldier's sword, the Christian's chart. It should fill the memory, rule the heart, and guide the feet."[1]

RELIABILITY

One of the most interesting studies you could do is on the topic of the Bible's reliability. Is the Bible we have today really God's Word? Is it accurate? Has it been added to? Can you trust it? In my own study I have found three primary things that point to its reliability: its transmission, its translation, and its confirmation.

Your Bible is regarded by theologians and historians as one of the most accurately transmitted texts of all times. The original copies of the Old Testament date back to the time of Moses (1405 B.C.) through the time of Malachi (400 B.C.), and we have grounds for confidence that today's Bible is an accurate translation. In 1947 near the Dead Sea, a number of scrolls were discovered that date back to the second and first centuries B.C. These scrolls, which contained all the books of the Old Testament except Esther, were found to be extremely accurate.[2]

In addition, the Hebrew text we have today has been checked with the Septuagint translation (a Greek translation of the Old Testament dating to the middle of the third century), the Aramaic Targums (paraphrases and quotes of the Old Testaments, quotations in early Christian writings), and the Latin translation of Jerome (A.D. 400), which was made directly from the Hebrew text of his day. All of these, when compared, give us confidence that the Hebrew text we have today of the Old Testament is indeed accurate.[3]

The New Testament is the best attested document of all ancient writings. More than 5,000 manuscripts of the New Testament exist today;[4] at least 8,000 manuscripts of the Latin Vulgate (common Latin versions of the New Testament);[5] and more than 36,000 quotations of the New Testament in the Church Fathers (translations dating from the third century).[6]

Some fragments of Bible manuscripts date to as early as A.D. 130.[7] These facts, coupled with the scholarly work that has been done to check the accuracy of the texts, assure us of the reliability of the Bible.

As you probably know, your Bible is a translation of the original writings: Hebrew in the Old Testament (except for small parts in Aramaic) and Greek in the New Testament. Thanks to qualified translators, you are able to read the Bible in

English today. A few of the more popular translations published in past years are:

- *King James Bible* (Authorized)—1611
- *American Standard Version*—1901
- *Berkeley Version*—1945
- *Revised Standard Version*—1946
- *New American Standard Bible*—1960
- *New English Bible*—1970
- *New International Version*—1973
- *New King James Bible*—1979

Each of these translations seeks to translate the Greek or Hebrew text exactly as it is written, word by word. Although scholars may question the meaning of a word here or there, each of these can be trusted as a reliable translation of God's Word.

Others have published Bible paraphrases in the simple speech of our everyday life. In a paraphrase, the premium is on readability for twentieth-century society. Instead of translating words exactly, the focus is on translating thoughts or ideas. Although you may find a paraphrase helpful as an introduction to Bible reading, I would not recommend it for serious study. The more a translation moves in the direction of a paraphrase, the greater the danger of distortion of the text. A few examples of paraphrases are:

- *The New Testament in Modern English*—1958
- *Good News for Modern Man*—1966
- *The Living Bible*—1971

A third factor supporting the Bible's reliability is the confirmation of archaeology. Nelson Glueck, a renowned Jewish archaeologist, wrote, "It may be stated categorically that no archaeological discovery has ever controverted a biblical

17

reference.''[8] Millar Burrows, of Yale, adds: "On the whole, archaeological work has unquestionably strengthened confidence in the reliability of the Scriptural record.''[9]

For example, in Greek, Acts 17:6 uses the title *politarchs* to refer to the civil authorities of Thessalonica. It was assumed by some, at one time, that Luke's reliability as a historian was questionable because *politarch* could not be found in classical literature. However, in recent years archaeological finds have uncovered at least nineteen inscriptions that make use of this title. In fact, five of these inscriptions are in reference to Thessalonica.

Archaeology has further substantiated the reliability of the New Testament. Sir William Ramsey, who is regarded as one of the greatest archaeologists to ever have lived, said of the book of Acts, "As an authority for the topography, antiquities and society of Asia Minor, it was gradually borne upon me that in various details the narrative shared marvelous truth.''[10]

Thanks to transmission, translation, and archaeological confirmations, the Bible can be trusted as reliable in communicating God's Word to us. Your Bible is an invaluable book, meant to be read and studied so that God might change your life.

The story is told of two friends who were discussing books one day. One was a rare-book collector, while his friend viewed old books as clutter to be thrown out. During their conversation the friend mentioned he had recently thrown out some old books that were in his attic.

"Old books?" The collector's voice changed. "You threw away old books—?"

"Yes," the friend replied, "in fact one was a big, old Bible."

"A big, old Bible?" the collector asked. "What kind of big, old Bible?"

"I don't know. It said *Guten*-something on it."

"A Gutenberg Bible?" the book collector shouted. "You

TUNE-UP 1

1. W. E. Gladstone once said, "The Bible is stamped with a specialty of origin, and an immeasurable distance separates it from all competitors." Based upon your reading of this section's material, name three characteristics of the Bible that would support Gladstone's statement.

A. Its C _____ .
B. Its A _____ .
C. Its R _____ .

2. Match the characteristics listed above with the following verses.

"The law of the Lord is
perfect, restoring the
soul; the testimony of
the Lord is sure, making   _____
wise the simple"
(Psalm 19:7).

"But know this first of
all, that no prophecy . . . was
ever made by an act of
human will, but men moved
by the Holy Spirit spoke   _____
from God" (2 Peter 1:20, 21).

"Thy words were found and
I ate them, and Thy words
became for me a joy and   _____
the delight of my heart"
(Jeremiah 15:16).

3. The Old Testament was originally written in
_____ and _____

---

4. The New Testament was originally written in _____.

5. Before you go on to the next section, commit to memory 2 Peter 1:20, 21 (*see* above). These two verses will remind you of the impeccable character of the Word of God.

(The answers to all Tune-up questions are in Chapter Ten " Specifications.")

---

threw out a Gutenberg Bible? The first book ever printed with movable type? A book that dates back to the fifteenth century? A book that is on the market today for twenty million dollars? You threw out a Gutenberg Bible?"

"Well," the friend replied, "this one I'm sure wasn't worth that much, especially since somebody named M. Luther had scribbled stuff all through it!"

Don't ever make the mistake of not seeing the Bible for what it's worth. It alone is the one book meant to change your life forever.

NOTES

1. F. F. Selle and Ewald Plass, *Quotations and Illustrations for Sermons* (Saint Louis: Concordia Publishing House, 1951), 20.
2. L. Archer Gleason, *A Survey of Old Testament Introduction* (Chicago: Moody Press, 1964), 37–42.
3. Josh McDowell, *Evidence That Demands a Verdict* (San Bernardino: Campus Crusade for Christ, 1972), 61–63.
4. Bruce M. Metzger, *The Text of the New Testament* (Oxford: Oxford University Press, 1968), 36.
5. A. T. Robertson, *Introduction to the Textual Criticism of the New Testament* (Nashville: Broadman Press, 1925), 29.

6. Norman L. Geisler and William E. Nix, *A General Introduction to the Bible* (Chicago: Moody Press, 1968), 353, 354.

7. Ibid., 268.

8. Nelson Glueck, *Rivers in the Desert: History of Neteg* (Philadelphia: Jewish Publications Society of America, 1969), 31.

9. Millar Burrows, *What Mean These Stones?* (New York: Bobbs-Merrill, 1960), 1.

10. McDowell, *Evidence That Demands a Verdict*, 73.

TWO

GETTING TO KNOW YOUR CAR

One of the first things we did when we brought our newly purchased car home was to look it over. I checked the specifications; Bernice checked to see how many grocery bags would fit in the back; and our children checked out the power windows! It was a lot of fun. The more we looked at it, the more we appreciated what we had purchased.

In a similar way, in order for you to fully appreciate your Bible, you need to get acquainted with it. It is comprised of sixty-six books. In their original form, the Hebrew and Greek manuscripts were written without chapter or verse divisions. These books grew together in the course of the centuries, through the guiding hand of God, to become the Bible we have today.

Thirty-nine of these books form the Old Testament. They were written before Christ, prior to 400 B.C. The Old Testament reveals why man needs a Savior. Since the Garden of Eden (Genesis 3), when man separated himself from God by "having it his way," he has needed Jesus Christ. The promise of the Old Testament is that one day the Messiah (Jesus) would come and provide the way back to God.

The New Testament consists of the remaining twenty-seven books. They were written following Christ's death and resurrection, after A.D. 30. They reveal the one and only way by which man can have an eternal relationship with God— through Jesus Christ. The New Testament tells us that Jesus is "the way, and the truth, and the life; no one comes to the Father, but through [Him]" (John 14:6). Philip, who later became one of Christ's twelve apostles, said: "We have found Him of whom Moses in the Law and also the Prophets wrote, Jesus of Nazareth" (John 1:45). The New Testament goes on to describe Christ's birth, childhood, life, death, resurrection, ascension, and promised coming return.

Have you found Jesus Christ? If you have, you will want to spend many hours in both Old and New Testament, getting to know Him in a personal way. As you do, the Bible promises you will actually become more like Him (2 Corinthians 3:18).

Whether you read the Old or New Testament, you will find the format of each individual book is like any other book, with chapters that are broken down into paragraphs. Within these chapters are sentences that form the verses.

Unlike a novel, the Bible is not an unbroken chain of historical events from beginning to end or from book to book. After you have gone through Ezra, Nehemiah, and Esther, the chain of events breaks off. From there on, the chronological sequence is intertwined in numerous books (that is, the book of Proverbs was most likely written during the pe-

TUNE-UP 2

Look up John 5:24 in your Bible.

1. Find John by looking up the page number in the table of contents. Turn there.
2. Find chapter 5.
3. Find verse 24.
4. Write the verse here: _____
_____
_____
_____

riod described in 1 Kings 4:32). It is best to see the Old Testament and New Testament order as primarily grouped according to topic and type of writing.

In the Old Testament there are four major groups: the Pentateuch (which means "five-fold vessel" and refers to the first five books of the Bible), followed by twelve historical books, five poetical books, and seventeen prophetical books. Two groups are distinguished among the prophetical books: the major prophets (the five longer books from Isaiah to Daniel) and the minor prophets (the twelve shorter books from Hosea to Malachi). The following chart outlines these groupings.

5	12	5	17
Pentateuch	Historical	Poetical	Prophetical
Genesis to Deuteronomy	Joshua to Esther	Job to Song of Solomon	Isaiah to Malachi
Historical Narrative		Poetry	Prophecy

25

TUNE-UP 3

Using your Old Testament table of contents:

1. What are the five books of the Pentateuch?

_____   _____
_____   _____
_____

2. What are the remaining twelve historical books?

_____   _____
_____   _____
_____   _____
_____   _____
_____   _____
_____

3. What are the five poetical books?

_____   _____
_____   _____
_____

4. What are the seventeen prophetical books?

_____   _____
_____   _____
_____   _____
_____   _____
_____   _____
_____   _____
_____   _____
_____

5. These equal a grand total of _____ books.

Historically the Old Testament is an account of several stages of Jewish history. Although in some cases it is difficult to be precise about the dates of these stages in biblical history, I have included dates that are accepted by many conservative scholars.

CREATION STAGE

Genesis 1–11.
From the birth of man to his fall.
Main actors: Adam, Noah.
Main actions: Creation, fall, flood, tower of Babel.

PATRIARCHAL STAGE

Genesis 12–50 and Job (2165–1805 B.C.).
The Jewish nation is born and moves to Egypt.
Main actors: Abraham, Isaac, Jacob, Joseph.
Main actions: Beginning of Hebrew nation; giving of Abrahamic covenant; Jews move to Egypt.

EXODUS STAGE

Exodus to Deuteronomy (1805–1406 B.C.).
Israel's bondage in Egypt and forty years of wandering in the wilderness after release.
Main actors: Moses, Aaron.
Main actions: Deliverance from Egypt; building the tabernacle; giving of the law; failure in the wilderness.

CONQUEST STAGE

Joshua (1406–1383 B.C.).
The Jewish people return to their homeland.
Main actors: Joshua, Caleb, Rahab.
Main actions: Conquest of the land; division of the land.

JUDGES STAGE

Judges to 1 Samuel 7 (1383–1043 B.C.).
While in their homeland, the Jews fall prey to habitual cycles of sin.
Main actors: Barak, Deborah, Gideon, Samson, Ruth, Eli, Samuel.
Main actions: Seven cycles of sin, servitude, supplication, salvation, and silence.

UNITED KINGDOM STAGE

First Samuel 8 to 1 Kings 11 (1043–931 B.C.); 1 Chronicles 1 to 2 Chronicles 9; Psalms to Song of Solomon.
Under three kings, Israel experiences one hundred twenty years of prosperity.
Main actors: Saul, David, Solomon.
Main actions: Saul's jealousy; David's anointing; Solomon's wisdom; first temple constructed.

CHAOTIC KINGDOM STAGE

First Kings 12 to 2 Kings; 2 Chronicles 10–36 (931–636 B.C.); Obadiah (850–840); Joel (841–834); Jonah (785–750); Amos (760–753); Hosea (760–700); Isaiah (739–681); Micah (735–700); Nahum (650–620).
Due to harsh taxation policies, the kingdom divided into northern and southern parts. The north had nineteen kings, of which none were God-fearing. The south had twenty kings, and eight served God.
Main actors: Jeroboam, Rehoboam, Elijah, Elisha.
Main actions: Israel's tragic civil war. Capture of northern kingdom by the Assyrians.

CAPTIVITY STAGE

Daniel (605–536 B.C.); Ezekiel (593–560).
After habitual sin and numerous prophetic warnings, the southern kingdom is taken into exile at Babylon for seventy years.
Main actors: Daniel, Nebuchadnezzar, Shadrach, Meshach, Abed-nego.
Main actions: Babylonian captivity of southern kingdom; deliverance of Daniel and his friends; first temple destroyed; Babylon's fall.

RETURN STAGE

Ezra (440–438 B.C.); Esther (478–463); Nehemiah (445–415); Haggai (520–504); Zechariah (520–508); Malachi (427–408).
With the decree of Cyrus, the Jews are permitted to return to their land.
Main actors: Cyrus, Zerubbabel, Ezra, Esther, Nehemiah.
Main actions: Deliverance of the Jews in Persia; Cyrus's decree; construction of the second temple; rebuilding of Jerusalem's walls.[1]

Turning to the New Testament, it, too, is arranged primarily by content. The first five books are historical narratives. The next twenty-one are letters; the last is prophetical.

Historical	Expositional	Prophetical
Matthew to Acts	Romans to Jude	Revelation
Narration	Interpretation	Prophecy

29

TUNE-UP 4

Number the stages of Old Testament Jewish history in chronological order.

_____ Conquest Stage

_____ Captivity Stage

_____ Patriarchal Stage

_____ United Kingdom Stage

_____ Exodus Stage

_____ Return Stage

_____ Judges Stage

_____ Creation Stage

_____ Chaotic Kingdom Stage

Here is another simple way to understand the contents of the New Testament:

THE CHRIST OF GOD (4 BOOKS)

Author, Matthew: Matthew.

Author, Mark: Mark.

Author, Luke: Luke.

Author, John: John.

THE CHURCH OF GOD (1 BOOK)

Author, Luke: The book of the Acts.

THE CORRESPONDENCE OF GOD (22 BOOKS)

Author, Paul: Galatians; 1 and 2 Thessalonians; 1 and 2 Corinthians; Romans; Ephesians; Colossians; Philemon; Philippians; 1 and 2 Timothy; Titus.

Author, John: 1, 2, and 3 John; Revelation.
Author, Peter: 1 and 2 Peter.
Author, James: book of James.
Author, Jude: book of Jude.
Author, unknown: book of Hebrews.

Together, both the Old and New Testaments form one book intended by God to be the means whereby He can bridge the gap between Himself and man. Through the Bible, God communicates His story, which centers on Jesus Christ. God's intended purpose in revealing to us His mind and will (Isaiah 55:1–11) is to have an immediate and lasting impact on the attitudes and actions of man.

I have found in my personal study that once I grasped the overall perspective, as I have given it to you here, it opened God's Word to me in a more meaningful way. A simple understanding of a few historical facts will be a tremendous help in your Bible study.

This is illustrated by an experience of Charles Lindbergh. On one of his early flights he lost a valuable instrument overboard. He watched it fall and land in the dense fields below. Later he landed a smaller plane in the general vicinity, and scoured the area by foot in search of the instrument, but to no avail. He resorted to a simple expedient. Taking off his coat, he spread it on a bush, and returned to the air. From the air he saw both the coat and the instrument, and he made some mental notes of relationship and bearing. Landing again, he walked to the coat, but still could not find the instrument. So he moved the coat to another bush and repeated the sighting from the air. With this additional bearing he was able finally to locate the instrument.[2]

In a similar way, if you commit to memory this historical overview, or keep this guide handy as you study, these facts will greatly enhance your ability to find the meaning of God's Word.

═══TUNE-UP 5═══

Using your New Testament table of contents, answer the following questions:

1. What are the five historical books?

_____   _____

_____   _____

_____

2. What are the twenty-one expositional books?

_____   _____

_____   _____

_____   _____

_____   _____

_____   _____

_____   _____

_____   _____

_____   _____

_____   _____

_____

3. What is the one prophetical book?

_____

4. These equal a grand total of _____ books.

NOTES

1. Irv Busenitz, Talbot Theological Seminary, "Old Testament Survey Class Notes," 1978.
2. Irving L. Jensen, *Enjoying Your Bible* (Chicago: Moody Press, 1969), 45.

THREE

THE FIRST
LAW OF DRIVING

If you are like me, when you get something new, you want to use it right away! But if it is a car, and especially your first car, there are certain laws you must know and be willing to obey before you can use it. They will add to your safety and will keep you out of a lot of trouble. One essential law states very simply that in order to operate an automobile, you must first have a valid driver's license, and you must keep it with you while you are driving.

Unfortunately many people—with very good intentions— have anxiously jumped into studying their Bibles and ended up getting themselves into trouble because they were not aware of, or failed to keep, one essential law: the law of literal interpretation.

One of the greatest dangers you face when you study God's Word is the danger of distorting the text to mean something it was never intended to mean. There is an ever-present tendency to read into the text something that is not there. This happens every time you distort the objective meaning of the text in order to make it say something that suits your own personal interests or bias. At that point, the authority of God's Word has been nullified and you become the authority.

Biblical scholars make a necessary distinction between what is called *exegesis* and *eisegesis*. Exegesis comes from a Greek word that means "to guide out of." To *exegete* Scripture is to get out of it the meaning that is there—no more and no less. On the other hand, *eisegesis* means "to guide into." In terms of interpretation, it means to read into the text something that is not there at all.

For example: If you were reading through the book of Isaiah and came across Isaiah 11:6, 7, what would you say it means? It says: "The wolf will dwell with the lamb, and the leopard will lie down with the kid, and the calf and the young lion and the fatling together. . . . Also the cow and the bear will graze."

Those who have interpreted this eisegetically have suggested a whole host of meanings for these verses. Some say the wolf is the United States, the lion Britain, the bear Russia—you get the idea. I don't think that is what this passage means. The exegetical approach suggests it simply means there is a day coming when the curse will be removed from the earth and the animals will be at peace with one another.

As you can see from the above example, eisegesis is subjective. Exegesis is objective and demands literal interpretation.

Our task is to *exegete* the Word of God—to interpret it literally. William Tyndale hits the nail on the head when he says,

Thou shalt understand, therefore, that the Scripture hath but one sense, which is the literal sense. And that literal sense is the root and ground of all, and the anchor that never faileth, whereunto if thou cleave thou canst never err or go out of the way. And if thou leave the literal sense, thou canst not but go out of the way. Nevertheless, the Scripture uses proverbs, similitudes, riddles, or allegories, as all other speeches do; but that which the proverb, similitude, riddle, or allegory signifieth is ever the literal sense, which thou must seek out diligently.[1]

The term *literal* comes from the Latin word *litera*, meaning "letter." To interpret something literally is to pay attention to the letters and words that are used. Though the Bible is a unique book, it is still subject to the laws of grammar: A noun remains a noun, a verb remains a verb. Its meaning can therefore be derived from an understanding of the normal rules of grammar, speech, syntax, and context.

In this light, one can see that the Bible is not too difficult for the ordinary person to understand. One does not require seminary training in order to interpret its meaning. It is not too heavy, too deep, or too profound.

In the chapters that follow, I will give you some specific

═══ TUNE-UP 6 ═══

Do you know the difference between *exegesis* and *eisegesis*?

1. To get out of a passage the meaning that is there = _____.

2. To read into the passage something that is not there = _____.

principles to help you make correct literal interpretations. At this point it is important for you to note that there are two ways to communicate literal truth. The first is through a plain literal statement, where the literal interpretation is found in the explicit meaning of the words. The second is through a figurative literal statement. Here the literal interpretation is found in the specific intention of the figure.

Second Chronicles 16:9 illustrates the difference. It says, "For the eyes of the Lord move to and fro throughout the earth that He may strongly support those whose heart is completely His." If this verse were meant to be interpreted in a plain literal sense, then God must have eyeballs that rotate the earth. That would be irreconcilable with what we know about God (that is, He is a spirit. See John 4:24.). In this passage, God is described in a figurative literal statement saying God knows who is devoted to Him.

In chapter seven I will give you some further assistance in interpreting figuratively literal statements.

At this point, I would ask you to make a firm resolution to understand the literal meaning whenever you are studying the Bible. Only by understanding the literal meaning of the passage will you be able to understand its significance and application.

Whether you are studying a large section of the Bible or one verse and its details, you should always strive to be accurate in your interpretation. The authority of God's Word is derived from a correct understanding of God's Word. You need to study the Bible with as much care and precision as is humanly possible.

Your task is to understand, through a process of literal interpretation, the meaning that was expressed by the speaker or writer of God's Word.

When I ask my oldest son to take out the trash, I mean one thing: I want him to go over to the trash bag, pick it up, take it out the door, walk to the garbage can, dump it in, and then come back into the house. My intention is singular, and "take out the trash" is to be taken literally. I am not asking him to "think about taking the trash out." As ridiculous as that sounds, much of the church today does that in their interpretation of the Bible. Instead of accepting the miracles or teachings of Jesus, they change them to mean something else. For instance, they would say that Jesus did not miraculously feed the five thousand but simply drew out of the crowd a latent spirit of generosity. When they saw the boy share his lunch, they followed his example by pulling their meals out from under their robes. The problem with this interpretation is that the passage does not say that!

Augustine has suggested the following interpretation for the parable of the Good Samaritan (*see* Luke 10:30–37):[2]

> By the certain man who went down from Jerusalem to Jericho, Adam himself is meant.
>
> Jerusalem is the heavenly city of peace, from whose blessedness Adam fell.
>
> Jericho means the moon, and signifies our mortality, because it is born, waxes, wanes, and dies.
>
> Thieves are the devil and his angels . . .
>
> Who stripped him, namely of his immortality . . .
>
> And beat him, by persuading him to sin . . .
>
> And left him half-dead, because in so far as man can understand and know God, he lives, but in so far as he is wasted and oppressed by sin, he is dead; he is therefore called half-dead.
>
> The priest and Levite who saw him and passed by signify the priesthood and ministry of the Old Testament, which could profit nothing for salvation.
>
> *Samaritan* means "guardian," and therefore the Lord Himself is signified by this name.
>
> The binding of the wounds is the restraint of sin.
>
> Oil is the comfort of good hope.
>
> Wine is the exhortation to work with fervent spirit.

The beast is the flesh in which He deigned to come to us.

Set upon the beast is belief in the incarnation of Christ.

The inn is the Church, where travellers are refreshed on their return from pilgrimage to their heavenly country.

The morrow is after the Resurrection of the Lord.

The two pence are either the two precepts of love, or the promise of this life and of that which is to come.

The innkeeper is the Apostle Paul.

As you can see, at the point one opts for any interpretation other than the literal interpretation, he opens the floodgates for theological chaos. Then who is to say what is true and what is not true in God's Word?

A word of caution may be useful here. There is a temptation in literal interpretation to push the application of its meaning beyond its original intent. It is important to understand the cultural and historical setting (discussed in chapter five) when applying the Bible's teaching to your life. This will ensure a correct application.

Yet it should be our goal to determine the literal usual and ordinary sense of the word or passage. This means that every passage will have one literal meaning. And that is the interpretation that we are to seek.

NOTES

1. William Tyndale, *Works*, vol. 1 (Cambridge: Parker Society Publication, 1860), 304.
2. Quoted in Herbert Lockyer, *All the Parables of the Bible* (Grand Rapids: Zondervan Publishing House, 1963), 20.

FOUR

STARTING YOUR CAR

Once you purchase a car and have a license to drive it, you can hardly wait to get in and go somewhere. But in order to do that, you must have a key. It will not only unlock the door for you and allow you to get into the car, but it will also start your car. Without that key, you will never be able to enjoy the full benefits of your new car.

The key that gets your study of God's Word started is careful observation. To begin with, if you are going to study a particular book in the Bible, first read the entire book before any portion of it is studied. As you read, do not stop and try to figure out what individual passages mean—just get acquainted with what the entire passage says. The purpose of this reading and rereading is to become thoroughly acquainted with the text. It may also be helpful to read the text in two or three different translations. For instance, look at how seeing 1 Corinthians 13:4, 5 in three different translations gives you a good start on understanding its meaning:

King James Version	*New American Standard Version*	*New International Version*
Charity suffereth long,	Love is patient	Love is patient
and is kind;	love is kind,	love is kind
charity envieth not;	and is not jealous,	It does not envy,
charity vaunteth not itself,	love does not brag,	it does not boast,
is not puffed up,	and is not arrogant	it is not proud
Doth not behave itself unseemly,	does not act unbecomingly;	It is not rude,
seeketh not her own,	it does not seek its own,	it is not self-seeking
is not easily provoked,	is not provoked,	it is not easily angered,
thinketh no evil.	does not take into account a wrong suffered.	it keeps no record of wrongs.

As you read, it is vital to observe carefully what is being said. Your observations at this point will help you to interpret what is said later. Like a sponge, your goal should be to absorb everything before you.

To assist you in making these observations, you will need to write down your findings as you go. Otherwise, unless you have a photographic memory, you will not be able to retain the things you see as you study. Record your interpretations. Underline key words and phrases in your Bible. Professor Louie Agassiz of Harvard said, "The pencil is one of the best eyes." Use it every time you study. Wilbur M. Smith, a man who has committed his life to the study of God's Word, says it well:

> We are now going to suggest something that so few Bible teachers seem to find it necessary to recommend. We believe it is one of the most essential aspects of personal, devotional Bible Study. We refer to the making of notes. If each young Christian would have a little notebook and actually write down, morning by morning, what the Lord gives out of the verse he or she is meditating upon, it would be found that thoughts would be clarified, the profit derived from Bible Study would be greatly increased, and a definite record of the things that the Holy Spirit has taught from day to day, or from week to week, would be had in permanent form.[1]

Here are some key things you will want to be looking for as you read.

THE LITERARY FORM

This is the type of writing an author uses to express his message. It influences the way his words are understood. There are three primary types:

1. *Prose* is straightforward language, narrative, or didactic teaching.
2. *Poetry* is most often used in a figurative way. Hebrew poetry is characterized by a rhyme of ideas rather than a rhyme

of sounds. Because of this, it is often hard to pick out of an English translation of the Bible. For this reason, the newer translations place poetry in verse form so it can be distinguished easily from prose. Numbers 6:22–26 (NIV) is a good example of this format.

The Lord said to Moses, "Tell Aaron and his sons, This is how you are to bless the Israelites. Say to them:

> " ' "The Lord bless you
> and keep you;
> the Lord make his face shine
> upon you
> and be gracious to you;
> the Lord turn his face toward
> you and give you peace." ' "

The rhymes in this passage are the phrases "keep you," "gracious to you," and "give you peace." They are used poetically to mean the same thing.

3. *Prophecy* is found throughout the Bible. Often these passages are steeped in many figures of speech, symbols, and so forth.

═══ TUNE-UP 7 ═══

Match the following verses with their literary forms:

Prose	John 2:18, 19
Poetry	Matthew 4:18
Prophecy	Psalm 46:7

THE GENERAL STRUCTURE

In order to communicate ideas, words must be related. The way an author arranges his ideas usually will communicate his purpose in writing. Various structural units must be considered, such as phrases, clauses, verses, paragraphs, and chapters. As you are reading, look for:

- *commands to obey*
- *questions to be answered*
- *sins to avoid*
- *promises to claim*
- *logical cause-and-effect sequences (if, then)*
- *connections or linking words (and, but, for, since, therefore)*
- *contrasts and comparisons (like, as)*
- *illustrations*

One method of noting the general structure is to mark a text with various symbols. This will help draw out the flow and meaning of the passage. For instance, using the symbols in Tune-up 8, Philippians 4:4–7 and Proverbs 3:5–10 would look like this:

Rejoice in the Lord always; again I will say, rejoice! Let your forbearing spirit be known to all men. The Lord is near. (Be anxious for nothing,) (but in everything by prayer and supplication with thanksgiving let your requests be made known to God.)(And) the peace of God, which surpasses all comprehension, shall guard your hearts and your minds in Christ Jesus.

(Trust in the Lord with all your heart,) (and do not lean on your own understanding.) In all your ways acknowledge Him, (and)He will make your paths straight. [Do not be wise in your own eyes;] Fear the Lord and [turn away from evil.] It will be healing to your body, (and) refreshment to your bones. Honor the Lord from your wealth, (and) from the first of all your produce; So your barns will be filled with plenty, (and) your vats will overflow with new wine.

═══════════ TUNE-UP 8 ═══════════

As you read Colossians 3:1–7 in your Bible, mark it with the following symbols:

– – – – – = commands
[   ] = sins to avoid
⬭ = connections
(   ) = contrasts
▭▭▭▭| = cause and effect
_____ = promises

If this one was too easy for you, try Ephesians 1:15–23 for a real challenge.

THE GRAMMATICAL CONSTRUCTIONS

You need to note the subject, the main verb, and the object of the verb (if any). Verbs lie at the heart of understanding any given passage. Everything finds its place in relation to the verb. Remember:

- *The subject does the action.*
- *The verb describes the action.*

• *The object receives the action.*

Learning to diagram sentences in this simple format will help you master the content of any given passage.

Subject	Verb	Object
Children	obey	your parents.
John	baptized	Jesus.

In addition to taking note of these three grammatical constructions, it will also be helpful to note:

• *Pronouns—she, they, we*
• *Adjectives—small, timid, loud*
• *Adverbs—quickly, boldly*
• *Prepositions—in the room, by the sea*

═══ TUNE-UP 9 ═══

Diagram the following sentences:

1. "Husbands, love your wives" (Colossians 3:19).
2. "Wives, be subject to your husbands" (Colossians 3:18).
3. "Children, be obedient to your parents" (Colossians 3:20).

If you need to bone up on English grammar I would recommend the following two excellent sources. Both are written in such a way that you don't have to be an English major to understand them. However, by the time you get through them, you'll be better equipped to dig into the meat of God's Word.

William Strunk, Jr., and E. B. White, *The Elements of Style*, 3rd
    ed. (New York: MacMillan Publishing Co., 1979).
Lauri Kirszner and Stephen Mondell, *The Holt Handbook* (New
    York: Holt, Rinehart, Winston Publishing Co., 1986).

KEY OR UNKNOWN WORDS

An author will often repeat words, usually for emphasis.
Ephesians 4:4–6 says,

> There is one body and one Spirit, just as also you
> were called in one hope of your calling; one Lord, one
> faith, one baptism, one God and Father of all who is
> over all and through all and in all.

Also note words of emphasis, such as *truly, verily, behold,
indeed, finally, especially.* An example is found in John 3:3:
"Jesus answered and said to him, 'Truly, truly, I say to you,
unless one is born again, he cannot see the kingdom of God.' "

ANSWERS TO SIX BASIC QUESTIONS

- Who? *Are there people involved?*
- What? *Has something happened? Is an idea expressed?*
- Where? *Is the location identified?*
- When? *Is it possible to determine the time?*
- Why? *Is there a reason or purpose stated?*
- How? *What is the means by which things are being
  accomplished?*

Miles Coverdale wrote, in the preface to his 1535 English
translation of the Bible, these famous lines. They reinforce the
value of answering these six questions in your study.

> It shall greatly helpe ye to understande Scripture,
> if thou mark not only what is spoken or wrytten, but of

whom, and to whom, with what words, at what time, where, to what intent, with what circumstances, considering what goeth before and what followeth.

═══════TUNE-UP 10═══════

Read Acts 3:1–10 and answer the following questions:

1. Who are the three key characters? _____, _____, _____.

2. What miracle took place?_____ _____

3. What was the beggar's attitude after the miracle? _____

4. Where did it happen?_____
5. When did this occur?_____
6. How did it happen (that is, whose power)? _____

NOTES

1. Wilbur M. Smith, *Profitable Bible Study* (Boston: W. A. Wilde Co., 1939), 65–67.

PUTTING
MILEAGE ON

One week after we got our new car, we took a trip to the zoo in Santa Barbara. It was an hour's drive from our home, and was the first time we really got the car out on the road and experienced its benefits in full. Although it added 150 miles onto our odometer and cost us a few dollars for gas, the trip was well worth it. We really had a lot of fun together that day.

Similarly, you have to be willing to put a few miles into your study. It will cost you in terms of time, energy, and mental effort, but it will be well worth it.

After you complete your overall observations, the next logical step in studying God's Word is to determine the meaning of what you have observed. Your goal should be to determine what the author meant by what he said. To do this, your study must cover four areas.

STUDY THE CONTEXT

The word *context* comes from Latin (*con* meaning "together," *textus* meaning "woven"). It is used to describe something woven together and can be applied to a written document. It usually means the portions surrounding the passage you are studying. Without an understanding of the context, your evaluation will fall short with a pretext.

To help you understand what the Bible means by what it says, you will need to consider four contexts. They can be thought of as four concentric circles.

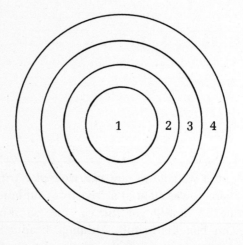

1. *The immediate context:* that which immediately precedes or follows a given word or principle (the surrounding paragraphs).

2. *The remote context:* the preceding or following chapter, or some other related part of the book.

3. *The book context:* evaluating the meaning in light of the book's outline and theme.

4. *The biblical context:* letting the Bible speak for itself and be its own commentary. Compare Scripture with Scripture. Look to see what other books have to say about the same event or principle.

For example, to truly understand what Paul meant by his statement "Love never fails" (1 Corinthians 13:8), you will need to look at how *love* is used in the verses surrounding verse 8 (the immediate context). Then you must determine how it is related to chapters 12–14 (the remote context). Next you need to see how it is used in the rest of the book of Corinthians (the book context). And finally you must see how it is used throughout the Old and New Testaments.

═══════TUNE-UP 11═══════

Study 1 Corinthians 13:8 in relationship to these four contexts. Remember, your goal is to determine what this verse means in its context.

1. In the immediate context, 1 Corinthians 13:8 means

_____

_____

_____

_____

2. In the remote context (1 Corinthians 12–14) 1 Corinthians 13:8 means_____

_____

_____

_____

_____

_____

3. In the book context, 1 Corinthians 13:8 means

_____

_____

_____

_____

_____

(*Suggested references:* 1 Corinthians 4:21; 8:1; 16:14, 24)
4. In the biblical context, 1 Corinthians 13:8 means

_____

_____

_____

_____

(*Suggested references:* Exodus 20:6; Leviticus 19:18; Deuteronomy 6:5; Psalm 97:10; Proverbs 10:12; Matthew 22:37–39; John 13:34, 35; 14:15; 15:13; 1 John 4:7–12)

STUDY THE WORDS

In order to understand what the Bible means by what it says, you must determine the correct meaning of the words. Words are the building blocks of thought, speech, and communication. Do not pass over a word you do not understand. The Word of God is too important to treat in a careless way. Stop and seek to determine its meaning.

1. *Study the word contextually:* The context will almost always tell you a great deal about the word.

2. *Study the word grammatically:* Note if the word is routine or significant (that is, usual or unexpected). Define it grammatically (singular or plural; past, present, or future), and remember the primary emphasis is on verbs.

3. *Study the word comparatively:* Check other translations

of the word when it is used in another context. If you have a study Bible, the cross-references will help you here. Also check other versions to see how the word was translated in the same verse.

4. *Study the word etymologically:* Discover its root meaning. Trace it back and find its historical beginning and see how it was used then (*see* chapter six).

5. *Study the word syntactically:* Check out how the word is used to form phrases, clauses, sentences, or paragraphs. Note the relationship of this word to other words in the sentence, trying to discern the meaning and flow of the passage.

■──────TUNE-UP 12──────

Read 1 Corinthians 13:3–8.

1. Contextually, *love* is equated with_____
_____
_____
_____

2. Contextually, *love* is contrasted with_____
_____
_____

3. Grammatically in this passage, *love* is used as a __ noun ____ verb. By definition in this passage, *love* is a ____ noun ____verb. That is indicated by_____
_____.

4. Syntactically, how does 1 Corinthians 13:8 relate to the immediate context (vv. 3–8)?_____
_____
_____
_____
_____

Remember, each individual word contributes something to the whole of the expressed content. The better you understand the individual words used in biblical statements, the better you will be able to understand the total message of Scripture.

STUDY THE HISTORICAL SETTING

To determine the correct meaning of what the Bible says, you must also interpret the words and context in harmony with the historical times of the author. Since Scripture originated in a historical context, it can be understood only in light of biblical history. Try to put yourself in the place of those who would have been the recipients of the Scripture you are studying. What would they have understood by the statement?

Insofar as possible, you should do your best to understand facts about the writer, the readers, the city, the church in that city, and other historical data. It would also be good to be aware of:

- *the specific time of writing*
- *the geography of the land*
- *the culture and customs*
- *the political situation*
- *the historical picture*

A proper understanding of the historical setting will lead to a proper application. Before asking, "What does the passage mean to me?" you need to ask, "What did the writer of this passage mean when he first wrote it?" As you study, seek to distinguish between historical cultural practices and eternal biblical principles.

For example, in 1 Corinthians 11:3–16, Paul says that when a woman prays or prophesies within the assembly she is to wear a veil as a symbol of submission. Did Paul intend women to wear veils in church throughout history?

TUNE-UP 13

Without the use of other references, you can find a great deal of information within 1 Corinthians to give you an understanding of the book's historical situation. Using the following verses, what conclusions can you draw?

1 Corinthians 2:1; 3:2 _____
_____
_____
_____

1 Corinthians 5:9 _____
_____
_____
_____

1 Corinthians 1:11–13 _____
_____
_____
_____
_____

1 Corinthians 7:1, 25 _____
_____
_____
_____

1 Corinthians 8:1–4 _____
_____
_____
_____

1 Corinthians 12:1 _____
_____
_____
_____

1 Corinthians 16:1_____

_____

_____

_____

A thorough study of the passage will reveal that there is a *principle* stated (submission) and a *practice* called for (wearing a veil). Therefore in applying this passage, one could:

1. Apply the principle of submission and its practice of wearing veils.

2. Ignore the principle of submission and its practice in veils.

3. Apply the principle of submission but ignore or replace the practice of veils with a new behavior that would express submission today.

How is the dilemma resolved? First, ask whether the principle is limited to first-century culture or is applicable to other cultures. (Here you could study 1 Corinthians 11:3 with Genesis 1 and 2.) Second, if the principle is applicable to today's culture, it must be determined if the practice is, too. One helpful question to ask is, "If the behavior were kept today, would it accurately express the principle stated [submission]?" And third, if the practice should be changed, how can this principle still be practiced today?

Stated simply, the key in finding principles is to be careful *not* to absolutize the relative (wearing veils) or to relativize the absolute (submission).

You will find that when you understand biblical principles in light of the historical setting, you will be able to accurately apply the passage to your life today.

STUDY THEOLOGICALLY

You must determine how what you have studied and concluded fits into the total pattern of God's revelation. God's revelation is progressive in the sense that He revealed Himself in various ways throughout history. He did not reveal everything about Himself at one time, nor did He tell everything to any one person. Thus in studying a topic in Scripture, you must investigate all Scripture as you gather together all the pieces of information and then draw an accurate conclusion. Your goal will be twofold:

1. To determine what has previously been revealed that scripturally relates to this area (analogy of Scripture). This is important in discovering the passage's meaning.

2. To determine what additional knowledge about the subject is available to you because of later revelation (analogy of faith). This is important in summarizing and drawing together conclusions from the passage.

Essential to this process will be a study of similar principles, themes, ideas, or teachings that can be found in other contexts. To do this, you will need to study:

1. *Word parallels.* This is where a parallel passage has the same words used in a similar connection. Compare Matthew 6:4–13 with Luke 11:2–4.

2. *Conceptual parallels.* These are passages in which likeness and identity exists not in words or phrases, but in facts, subjects, or doctrines. Compare Philippians 2:5–11 and Hebrews 2:9–18.

Fortunately there are aids to assist you in this process. Chapter six will acquaint you with them.

It might seem, from what I've written in chapters four and five, that being able to understand what the Bible means will

TUNE-UP 14

In order to gain a broader theological perspective on *love*, read John 13:1–15, 33–35 and 1 John 4:7–12. Draw out *one* principle from each passage that helps you in understanding 1 Corinthians 13:8.

1. _____

_____

_____

2. _____

_____

_____

depend strictly on your abilities to observe the text and study carefully. Fortunately this is not the case.

Successful Bible study is dependent on both you and God—God's enabling aptitude and your submissive attitude. Both aspects are described in 1 Corinthians 2:14: "A natural man does not accept the things of the Spirit of God; for they are foolishness to him, and he cannot understand them, because they are spiritually appraised."

Through the Holy Spirit, God gives you the aptitude to understand the Word of God. You will be able to make sense out of God's Word. Unlike the natural man, who looks at the Bible and sees it as foolishness, you will see God's Word for what it is. You will be able to understand its intended spiritual meaning.

In conjunction with God's enabling aptitude must be your submissive attitude. When you read or study God's Word, your attitude should be like David's. His prayer in Psalm 119:18

should also be yours: "Open my eyes, that I may behold wonderful things from Thy law." I find as I study it is essential to keep David's prayer foremost in my mind. You, too, must prayerfully ask God to show you from His Word what He would wish to be perpetually etched on your heart. As He does, willingly and prayerfully you should seek to make His Words a part of your life.

A submissive attitude will drive you to diligently study the Bible. Your goal will be to interpret it faithfully and apply it quickly. God's enabling aptitude makes the whole process of meaningful Bible study possible.

SIX

DEALER ASSISTANCE

Sooner or later you are going to need some help to keep your car running. Fortunately the manufacturer has realized that and has established service departments across the land that can give your car the special attention it will need. Whether it is a tune-up, touch-up, cleanup, or lineup, they can do it. They have the tools and the additional training to get the job done.

God has given us certain scholars who have invested their lives in the study of His Word. They are like a service department to us. After years of study, they have published books of commentaries, concordances, word studies, and so forth, to assist us in the process of understanding what the Bible means.

In this chapter I would like to introduce you to several books that could be an invaluable asset to your future Bible study. These books will assist you in studying the context, words, historical settings, and theology.

For the purpose of illustrating how you can use these sources, we will examine Luke 4:14, 15, which says:

> And Jesus returned to Galilee in the power of the Spirit; and news about Him spread through all the surrounding district. And He began teaching in their synagogues and was praised by all.

STUDYING THE CONTEXT

You will find in Bible bookstores several sources that will help you understand the biblical context. If you have a study Bible, the introduction to each book will be an invaluable source of information about the immediate, remote, book, and biblical contexts. Other Bible-overview books that have been published will give you information about the books, author,

━━━━━━━━TUNE-UP 15━━━━━━━━

Luke 4:14 says, "And Jesus returned to Galilee...." Using the above chart, answer the following questions:

1. Where was Jesus returning from?_____
2. What section of Scripture in Luke covers Jesus' Galilean ministry?_____
3. Luke 1 to 4:13 centered on the *advent* of Jesus. However, Luke 4:14–9:50 centers on the_____ of Jesus.
4. Jesus' ministry at this point was prominent in____ _____.

date written, historical setting, location, theme, purpose, and a brief synopsis of the contents of each chapter in the book.

Some of the books will introduce much of the help you need in the form of a chart. Here is an excellent overview of the book of Luke.[1]

Focus	Advent		Activities		Antagonism and Admonitions		Affliction	Authentication
	1 4:13	4:14 9:50	9:51 19:27	19:28 23	24
D I V I S I O N S	Identification of the Son of Man	Presentation of the Son of Man	Authority of the Son of Man	Ministry of the Son of Man	Rejection of the Son of Man	Teaching of the Son of Man	Suffering of the Son of Man	Resurrection of the Son of Man
	1 2	3:1–4:13	4:14 6	7 9:50	9:51 11	12 19:27	19:28 23	24
T O P I C S	Seeking the Lost					Saving the Lost		
	Miracles Prominent				Parables and Teaching Prominent			
	Presentation		Preaching			Passion		
Locations	Nazareth, Wilderness		Galilee		On the Way to Jerusalem		Jerusalem	
Time	5 B.C.–A.D. 33							

Your goal at this stage should be to gather as much information about the context as possible. Sources like the one above will assist you in your contextual study.

Another valuable resource to assist you in understanding the context is a Bible atlas. An atlas will help you locate geographically the cities you are studying and other pertinent information.

Of interest in our study is the fact that "Jesus returned to

Galilee . . . and news about Him spread through all the surrounding district.'' John 4:46–54 reveals that Jesus first went to the city of Cana. From there He traveled to Nazareth (Luke 4:16) and then into Capernaum (Luke 4:31). As you can see from the map below, an atlas will enhance your understanding of the historical setting.

REGION OF GALILEE[2]

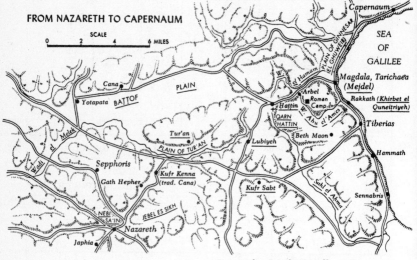

© 1955 by Rand McNally & Company

SUGGESTED RESOURCES

Bruce Wilkinson, *Talk Thru the Old Testament* (Nashville: Thomas Nelson Publishers, 1983).

Bruce Wilkinson, *Talk Thru the New Testament* (Nashville: Thomas Nelson Publishers, 1983).

STUDYING THE WORDS

A concordance will enable you to find out how and where a word is used through the whole Bible. An exhaustive concordance such as the *New American Standard Exhaustive Concordance* lists all or nearly all the times every word occurs in the Bible. Smaller concordances, such as *Cruden's,* list the primary occurrences of a word, but not all of them.

All Bible concordances list the words of the Bible in alphabetical order, along with verses that contain these words. Just as translations differ in their usage of words, so do concordances. If the translation of the Bible you use is King James, it would be best to refer to *Strong's Exhaustive Concordance, Young's Analytical Concordance* or *Cruden's Concordance. Nelson's Complete Concordance* is available for the Revised Standard Version. If you are studying out of the New American Standard translation, the *New American Standard Exhaustive Concordance* is best for you.

In Luke 4:15 the word *synagogue* is used. If you wanted to learn more about the usage of synagogues in the Bible, this is what you would find in an exhaustive concordance:[3]

SYNAGOGUES

all Galilee, teaching in their s,	Mt 4:23	4864
as the hypocrites do in the s and in	Mt 6:2	4864
they love to stand and pray in the s	Mt 6:5	4864
the villages, teaching in their s.	Mt 9:35	4864
and scourge you in their s;	Mt 10:17	4864
and the chief seats in the s,	Mt 23:6	4864
them you will scourge in your s,	Mt 23:34	4864
their s throughout all Galilee,	Mk 1:39	4864
and chief seats in the s,	Mk 12:39	4864
and you will be flogged in the s,	Mk 13:9	4864
He began teaching in their s and	Lk 4:15	4864
on preaching in the s of Judea.	Lk 4:44	4864
you love the front seats in the s,	Lk 11:43	4864
when they bring you before the s	Lk 12:11	4864
He was teaching in one of the s on	Lk 13:10	4864
places, and chief seats in the s,	Lk 20:46	4864
delivering you to the s and prisons,	Lk 21:12	4864

I always taught in s,	Jn 18:20	4864
asked for letters from him to the s	Ac 9:2	4864
began to proclaim Jesus in the s,	Ac 9:20	4864
word of God in the s of the Jews;	Ac 13:5	4864
he is read in the s every Sabbath."	Ac 15:21	4864
in the temple, nor in the s,	Ac 24:12	4864
I punished them often in all the s,	Ac 26:11	4864

In your concordance you will always find the word you are looking up in the top left corner of the list. In this case it is *synagogues*. An abbreviated form of the verses that have *synagogues* in them are listed in the order they occur in the Bible. The word *synagogues* is abbreviated with an s. This is typical of what you will find in your concordance.

In addition to references where the word *synagogues* is used in the Bible, you will see *4864* in the far right column. By looking up number 4864 in the back of your concordance, you would find the following:[4]

> *4864.* συναγωγή **sunagōgē**; from *4863; a bringing together,* by ext. *an assembling,* hence *a synagogue:*— assembly(1), synagogue(31), synagogues(24).

This added information will assist you in establishing a general meaning of the word and in grasping an understanding of the ways in which it is translated in your Bible.

As you can see, just a comparative study of the word *synagogues* in a concordance gives you a wealth of information on its usage in the Bible.

Additional sources are also available that will assist you in understanding key words. For example, Collin Brown's *The New International Dictionary of New Testament Theology* and Gerhard Kittel's *Theological Dictionaries* would give you an extensive examination of key words. Richard Trent's book *Synonyms of the New Testament* is also helpful. A. T. Robertson's *Word Pictures in the New Testament* is an excellent

══TUNE-UP 16══

Using the above Bible references and information, what insight have you gained about‚synagogues?_____

_____

_____

_____

source. One source I have found especially useful in tracing Old and New Testament words in their contexts is *Vine's Expository Dictionary of Old and New Testament Words.* Looking up the word *synagogue*, you find the following:[5]

SYNAGOGUE

SUNAGŌGĒ (συναγωγή), properly a bringing together (*sun*, together, *agō*, to bring), denoted (*a*) a gathering of things, a collection, then, of persons, an assembling, of Jewish religious gatherings, e.g., Acts 9:2; an assembly of Christian Jews, Jas. 2:2, R.V., "synagogue" (A. V., marg.; text, "assembly"); a company dominated by the power and activity of Satan, Rev. 2:9; 3:9; (*b*) by metonymy, the building in which the gathering is held, e.g. Matt. 6:2; Mark 1:21. The origin of the Jewish synagogue is probably to be assigned to the time of the Babylonish exile. Having no Temple, the Jews assembled on the sabbath to hear the Law read, and the practice continued in various buildings after the return. Cp. Ps. 74:8.

As you can see, if you were to take all that you have gleaned from these sources on synagogues, you could have a fairly thorough understanding of the synagogues Christ taught in in Galilee.

═══════TUNE-UP 17═══════

What further information do you gain from this source regarding synagogues?_____

_____

_____

_____

SUGGESTED RESOURCES

James Strong, *The Exhaustive Concordance of the Bible* (New York: Abingdon Press, 1961).

Robert L. Thomas, ed., *New American Standard Exhaustive Concordance of the Bible* (Nashville: Holman Press, 1981).

W. E. Vine, *Vine's Expository Dictionary of Biblical Words* (Nashville: Thomas Nelson Publishers, 1985).

STUDYING THE HISTORICAL SETTING

There are also books that will help you understand the historical situation. The more you know about the writer, the readers, the city, the church in that city, and other relevant historical data, the more apt you are to make a correct interpretation of the passage. Using the word *Galilee*, here is how Smith's bible dictionary would help you understand Galilee during the time of Christ.[6]

> **Gal'ilee** (*circuit*). In the time of our Lord all Palestine was divided into three provinces, Judea, Samaria and Galilee. Luke 17:11; Acts 9:31; Joseph. *B. J.* iii. 3. The latter included the whole northern section of the country, including the ancient territories of Issachar,

Zebulun, Asher and Naphtali. It is a remarkable fact that the first three Gospels are chiefly taken up with our Lord's ministrations in this province, while the Gospel of John dwells more upon those in Judea.

(*Galilee in the time of Christ.*—From Rev. Selah Merrill's late book (1861) with this title, we glean the following facts:

Size.—It is estimated that of the 6000 square miles in Palestine west of the Jordan, nearly one-third, almost 2000 square miles, belongs to Galilee.

Population.—The population is between 2,000,000 and 3,000,000. Dr. Merrill argues for the general correctness of Josephus' estimates, who says there were 204 cities and villages in Galilee, the smallest of which numbered 15,000 inhabitants.

Character of the country.—Galilee was a region of great natural fertility. Such is the fertility of the soil that it rejects no plant, for the air is so genial that it suits every variety. Here were found all the productions which made Italy rich and beautiful. Forests covered its mountains and hills, while its uplands, gentle slopes and broader valleys were rich in pasture, meadows, cultivated fields, vineyards, olive groves and fruit trees of every kind.

Character of the Galileans.—They were thoroughly a Jewish people. With few exceptions they were wealthy and in general an influential class.

The Galileans had many manufactures, fisheries, some commerce, but were chiefly an agricultural people. They were eminent for patriotism and courage, as were their ancestors, with great respect for law and order.)

A Bible dictionary like the *New Bible Dictionary* (which is an excellent source) will provide you with such information. Bible dictionaries list and explain words and subjects found in the Bible. Like an English dictionary, the words or subjects are arranged in alphabetical order and usually are printed in large, boldface type and set slightly into the left-hand margin so as to be easily found. The explanation that follows each heading should give you a broader understanding of the word or subject you are attempting to understand. Most Bible dictionaries summarize the intended biblical meaning but do not necessarily give many additional biblical references (as a concordance would).

TUNE-UP 18

What have you learned about:

1. Galilee's location? _____

_____

2. Galilee's size and population? _____

_____

3. Galilee's topography? _____

_____

4. Galilee's people? _____

_____

_____

STUDYING THEOLOGICALLY

Finally, there are books that will help you interpret the passage correctly in its immediate setting and the broader biblical context. Commentaries are valuable sources at every stage of your study.

Commentaries fall into three general categories:

1. *Exegetical commentaries.* These deal with the original languages of the text and attempt to explain grammatical and syntactical areas.

2. *Analytical commentaries.* These attempt to give the reader a well-balanced view of the entire passage. They deal with the historical setting and word studies, and they draw doctrinal inferences from the text.

3. *Devotional commentaries.* These seek to bring out practical inferences from the Scriptures.

If you are going to use a commentary to assist you in understanding the meaning of the passage, it is best to begin with an exegetical or analytical commentary. These will help you make a literal interpretation. Only look at devotional commentaries after you have a firm grasp of the passage and its proper interpretation.

When you are ready to purchase a commentary, here are a few things to keep in mind that will help you select one that is appropriate for your study and for you.

- *Does it use original languages?*
- *Does it deal with generalities only, or does it get specific?*
- *Can you understand it?*
- *Is it doctrinally sound (that is, what is its theological position)?*
- *Does it stick to the text, or does it wander?*
- *Does it present fresh material, or just the ideas of others?*
- *Does it make good use of history, archaeology, customs, and so forth?*

Going back to Luke 4:14, 15, you might want to consult a commentary to gain a broader perspective on the immediate passage and how it fits into other Scriptures. In the *New Testament Commentary on Luke,* which from my perspective is an analytical commentary, William Hendriksen writes:[7]

> As Luke here briefly summarizes the Great Galilean Ministry, particularly the teaching in which Jesus

was then engaged, it had the following characteristics. It was:

a. *Spirit endowed:* Jesus performed his task as One who was filled with the Holy Spirit, who had descended upon him in connection with his baptism and had been his Guide in the wilderness (3:22; 4:1);

b. *widely advertised:* the news about it and about him was spreading throughout the entire surrounding region;

c. *synagogue-centered:* see Matt. 4:23a, and for the history and importance of the synagogue see N.T.C. on Mark, pp. 74–76; and

d. *popular.* Note the words, "and he was praised by everybody." For further confirming evidence showing how the people flocked to hear Jesus' teaching (both in the synagogue and elsewhere) see Luke 4:22a, 32; 5:1; cf. Matt. 7:28, 29; 9:35, 36; 13:1, 2, 54; Mark 1:21, 22; 2:13; 4:1; etc. It should be borne in mind, however, that this popularity was by no means unqualified. At times those who at first were filled with enthusiasm became adversely critical and even antagonistic as soon as they began to realize that Christ's teaching conflicted with their prejudices, as this very chapter shows.

═══TUNE-UP 19═══

Using the above, what further things have you learned

1. About Christ's power? _____

_____

2. About Christ's popularity? _____

_____

3. About Christ's teaching? _____

_____

SUGGESTED RESOURCES

My personal conviction leads me to urge you to begin to build a Bible study library today. It may cost you a few dollars, but probably no more than you spent on your TV! Investing in excellent study books will enable you to benefit from the rich dividends of study in God's Word.

- Wycliffe Bible Commentary on the Whole Bible (*Chicago: Moody Press*).
- *Charles F. Pfeiffer and Everett F. Harrison*, Wycliffe Bible Commentary (*Chicago: Moody Press, 1962*).

For topical studies:

Orville J. Nave, ed., Nave's Topical Bible (*Chicago: Moody Press, 1974*).

Harold Monser, ed., Topical Index to the Bible (*Grand Rapids: Baker Book House, 1960*).

R. A. Torrey, Treasury of Scripture Knowledge (*Old Tappan: Fleming H. Revell Co., 1973*)

For doctrinal studies:

Everett F. Harrison, ed., Baker's Dictionary of Theology (*Grand Rapids: Baker Book House, 1978*).

Charles C. Ryrie, A Survey of Bible Doctrine (*Chicago: Moody Press, 1972*).

Lewis Sperry Chafer, Major Bible Themes (*Grand Rapids: Zondervan Publishing House, 1974*).

For church history:

Earle Erwin Cairns, Christianity Through the Centuries (*Grand Rapids: Zondervan Publishing House, 1954*).

Philip Schaff, History of the Christian Church, 8 vols. (*Grand Rapids: Wm. B. Eerdmans Publishing Co., 1950*).

Tim Dowley, ed., Handbook to the History of Christianity (*Grand Rapids: Wm. B. Eerdmans Publishing Co., 1977*).

For geographical and archaeological studies:

L. H. Grollenberg, compiler, Nelson's Atlas of the Bible (*New York: Thomas Nelson & Sons, 1956*).

> Emil G. Kraeling, Rand McNally Bible Atlas (*Chicago: Rand McNally, 1956*).
>
> J. A. Thompson, The Bible and Archaeology (*Grand Rapids: Wm. B. Eerdmans Publishing Co., 1962*).

Occasionally someone may say that it is evil to use scholarly references (commentaries, word studies, and so forth), since they are only man's thoughts, and we should not use them, only read the Bible. In one sense, they are right! The Bible should be your primary source when seeking an accurate interpretation.

However, you will also find it is sometimes necessary to seek further assistance in your interpretations. When you do, be careful! Not all the tools on the market are accurate or reliable. If you can, seek the advice of someone you respect prior to purchasing your Bible interpretation tools. Be discerning. Reference works are not infallible. When you are ready to make your purchase look for books that are:

1. *Biblically centered. Is the Bible central in deriving the passage's proper interpretation?*
2. *Objectively interpreted. Is the author's purpose to subjectively win you over to his position or to objectively present the evidences that you might decide?*
3. *Time tested. Newer products aren't always the best tools to buy. When was it published? Has it stood the test of time?*

I think you will find a few good tools to be a valuable asset to your study. C. H. Spurgeon discovered that and once said to those who objected to such a thought:

> Of course, you are not such wiseacres as to think or say that you can expound Scripture without assistance from the works of divines and learned men who

have laboured before you in the field of exposition. If you are of that opinion pray remain so, for you are not worth the trouble of conversion, and like a little coterie who think with you, would resent the attempt as an insult to your infallibility.

NOTES

1. Bruce Wilkinson, *Talk Thru the New Testament* (Nashville: Thomas Nelson Publishers, 1983), 29.
2. Emil G. Kraeling, *Rand McNally Bible Atlas* (New York: Rand McNally & Co., 1956), 372.
3. Robert Thomas, ed., *New American Standard Exhaustive Concordance.* (Nashville: Holman Press, 1981), 1194.
4. Ibid., 1685.
5. W. E. Vine, *Vine's Exhaustive Dictionary of New Testament Words* (Old Tappan: Fleming H. Revell, n.d.), 101.
6. William Smith, *A Dictionary of the Bible* (Grand Rapids: Zondervan Publishing House, 1948), 203.
7. William Hendriksen, *New Testament Commentary on Luke.* (Grand Rapids: Baker Book House, 1978), 248.

MINOR
TROUBLESHOOTING

I am not an expert mechanic by any means, but I do know enough about cars to be able to do minor troubleshooting. If the car will not start and the gas gauge is on E, I usually can ascertain that we are out of gas. If I turn on the headlights and only one comes on, I have found that if I replace a light bulb, I will solve the problem. It does not always take a professional mechanic to keep my car running smoothly.

The following material is here to help you do your own biblical troubleshooting. In the process of your study, it will not be long until you come across something that just does not make sense when interpreted in a plain literal way. For example, Jesus said, "I am the bread of life" (John 6:148). "I am the light of the world" (John 8:12). "I am the door of the sheep" (John 10:17).

If you take these three statements in a straightforward, literal way, you are forced to describe Jesus as bread, light, and a door.

Many such examples are found throughout Scripture. The psalmist writes, "The righteous man will flourish like the palm tree, He will grow like a cedar in Lebanon" (Psalm 92:12). Literally this says a righteous man is a palm tree.

These are examples of figurative language. Often in Scripture you will find an inanimate object used to describe a living being. It will stand out very clearly because the expression will be out of character with the thing described. More often than not, the context will tell you immediately whether the expression is meant to be taken figuratively or literally. Using the example of Psalm 92:12, the word *like* is used two times in comparing the righteous man to palm and cedar trees. This word immediately identifies this statement as a simile.

To help you troubleshoot in these areas, I have given you below a few principles that you should become familiar with. They will help you make correct interpretations. But remember, our law of literal interpretation still applies in these areas. Although the language may be figurative, it is still meant to convey a literal meaning. If someone said to me, "I'm going to put out your lights!" I would immediately understand that he meant to beat me up! He may have expressed it in a figurative way, but he meant one literal thing. In the same way, biblical figurative language is meant to be interpreted literally.

Here are a few principles that will help you troubleshoot in these areas.

PARABLES

The word *parable* means to throw or place by the side of, and carries the idea of placing one thing by the side of another for the purpose of comparison or illustration.

Parables are narrative in the sense that they contain a sequence of actions. They are true to life because they are within the realm of probability. They are designed to convey a specific point, rather than reiterate a historical situation. The purpose of the parable is to convey one specific point—one overall idea—so do not try to find a meaning behind each specific detail of the parable.

When Christ spoke in parables, His primary purpose was twofold: To conceal truth from those who were not responsive to it and to reveal truth to those who would respond.

When interpreting parables, you must be careful to:

1. Determine the one central truth the parable is attempting to teach.

2. Determine how much of the parable is interpreted by the Lord Himself (search the context).

3. Determine the specific problem in its immediate context (the cultural setting, and so forth). Why is He telling the parable?

4. Use the comparative rule. Compare the parable with any possible Old Testament association and with the parable as recited in one or more of the other Gospels.

FIGURATIVE LANGUAGE

More than two hundred types of figures have been distinguished in Scripture. Some of the more common ones are:

Simile: A formal comparison between two different or unlike things. Key words are *like* and *as. Examples:* Psalm 102:6; Isaiah 55:10, 11; Jeremiah 23:29.

Metaphor: A comparison in which one thing is described in terms of something else. *Examples:* Jeremiah 2:13; Hosea 13:8; Matthew 5:13, 14.

═══════TUNE-UP 20═══════

Turn to Matthew 7:24–27 and read the parable of the builders. Then answer the following questions.

1. What is the one central message of the parable?

_____

2. Did Jesus give an explanation of the parable?

_____

3. Why did He tell the parable? _____

_____

4. Does the account in Luke 6:47–49 give you any further insights?_____

_____

Allegory: An extended metaphor. An allegory uses words in a metaphoric sense, and its narrative, however supposable in itself, is manifestly fictitious. *Example:* John 15:1.

Irony: Words that convey an idea that is the exact opposite of what is intended. *Examples:* Job 12:1, 2; 1 Corinthians 4:8.

Hyperbole: An exaggeration to gain greater effect (hyper + bole = a throwing beyond). *Examples:* John 21:25; 2 Samuel 1:23; Psalm 6:6.

Personification: A thing, quality, or idea is represented as a person or an animal. *Examples:* Numbers 16:32; Matthew 15:34; Isaiah 40:9.

Paradox: An apparent contradiction. A statement may seem contradictory, but in reality is true. *Example:* Philippians 2:12, 13.

Proverb: This is a brief but wise saying meant to govern life in some aspect and worthy of consideration because it has proven valid through the tests of time and experience. *Examples:* Proverbs 26:4; 27:5, 6.

=====TUNE-UP 21=====

Using the definitions listed above, classify these verses as to the type of figurative language that is used.

1. Judges 7:12   _____
2. Matthew 5:13   _____
3. 1 Kings 18:27   _____
4. Mark 7:19   _____
5. Galatians 2:20   _____
6. Genesis 49:9   _____
7. Luke 4:23   _____
8. Habakkuk 3:10   _____

TYPOLOGY

A *type* is an Old Testament institution (tabernacle: Hebrews 9, 10); event (Passover: 1 Corinthians 5:7); person (Melchizedek: Genesis 14; Hebrews 5, 7); object (brazen serpent: Numbers 21; John 3:14); or animal (Passover lamb: John 1:29; 1 Corinthians 5:7), which has reality and purpose in biblical history but which by divine design illustrates and foreshadows something greater in the future.

Primarily there are two types of *types*. The first are referred to as *innate types*. These are specifically indicated as types in Scripture (Romans 5:19; Hebrews 5:10). Second, there are *inferred types*. These can be inferred as such because of the direct interchange of terminology or its manifest and evident analogies (1 Corinthians 5:7; 1 Peter 1:19).

In order to interpret types correctly, you must:

1. Look for the *basic* meaning of the symbol. The "law of first occurrence," or the first place a symbol occurs, is usually very helpful in gaining the basic meaning.

2. Realize that the physical or literal is often used to picture the spiritual.

3. Note the historical setting of the type.

4. Look for consistent use of a type in the Old Testament. But remember its interpretation must be consistent with New Testament truth.

5. Note the differences. Do not expect every detail to fit. Every analogy, by its very nature, falls short at the full reality.

6. Look for correspondence between the literal and figurative meaning. The symbolic meaning must correspond to the original literal meaning.

7. Never prove doctrine from types unless there is clear New Testament authority.

══TUNE-UP 22══

Read Exodus 12:1–13, 42–51 and 1 Corinthians 5:7. Outline three ways in which the Passover was a type of Christ.

1. _____

_____

2. _____

_____

_____

3. _____

_____

_____

PROPHECY

Here are some things to keep in mind when you are dealing with prophetic passages.

1. Does the natural sense make sense? If possible, interpret it literally (Isaiah 11).

2. Search the larger context to find a similar prophecy that might shed light (Isaiah 9:6).

3. Search the immediate context—words, phrases, time, place.

4. Does the New Testament indicate time of fulfillment? (Isaiah 9:1.)

5. Make sure the alleged New Testament fulfillment agrees with the prophecy in its details.

6. Continually strive to be objective.

POETRY

Unlike the poetry that we know, where words rhyme, in Hebrew poetry the thoughts and ideas rhyme, rather than the words. Most of the poetry in the Bible is composed of two lines the author carefully constructed to rhyme in thought. This is called *Hebrew parallelism.* An understanding of these types will help in interpreting poetry.

1. *Synonymous parallelism.* The second line expresses the same thought as the first. "The earth is the Lord's, and all it contains, the world, and those who dwell in it" (Psalm 24:1).

2. *Antithetic parallelism.* The second expresses a thought in contrast to the first line. "A gentle answer turns away wrath, but a harsh word stirs up anger" (Proverbs 15:1).

3. *Emblematic parallelism.* One line is literal, while the other is figurative. Look for a simile or metaphor. "As the deer pants for the water brooks, so my soul pants for Thee, O God" (Psalm 42:1).

4. *Stairlike parallelism.* Building on a thought or word. Usually a part of the first line is repeated as the remaining context builds up to a climax. "For it is not an enemy who reproaches me, then I could bear it; nor is it one who hates me

who has exalted himself against me, then could I hide myself from him. But it is you, a man my equal, my companion and my familiar friend'' (Psalm 55:12, 13).

═══TUNE-UP 23═══

In John 2:13–22, two specific prophecies are recorded. What are they?

1. _____

_____

2. _____

_____

How was Jesus' action in John 2:13–16 a fulfillment of the first prophecy?

_____

_____

_____

When was the second prophecy fulfilled?

_____

_____

_____

═══TUNE-UP 24═══

Categorize the following verses as to their type of parallelism.

1. Proverbs 25:24 _____
2. Psalm 29:1, 2 _____
3. Psalm 103:3 _____
4. Proverbs 14:18 _____

EIGHT

ENJOYING
YOUR CAR

As I write this chapter, I am in Portland, Oregon. My family and I are over one thousand miles from our home. Instead of flying here, we drove in our new car. What could have taken two hours took three days. Outside of a few normal mishaps, we had a lot of fun during the trip. In fact, yesterday I saw a bumper sticker that reminded me of our drive here. It said, "Are we having fun yet?" Not a bad question to ask, especially after riding in your car for three days with two boys under five years of age! Actually we really did enjoy our trip (the boys were miraculously well-behaved!) and many times found ourselves thanking God for our new car with so much room.

Unfortunately, some people are not having fun yet with their Bibles because they have not used them. Usually a person who has failed to enjoy his study of God's Word is one who has not learned to apply its message to his life. The next logical step after you have understood the meaning of God's Word is to use it in your personal life. Application is the end goal of Bible study. God did not give us His Word just so we would have something to study or talk about with other Christians, but rather that it might change our lives. We must obey the Bible if we are to continue to enjoy its benefits in our lives. David said in Psalm 19:7–11,

> The law of the Lord is perfect, restoring the soul; the testimony of the Lord is sure, making wise the simple. The precepts of the Lord are right, rejoicing the heart; the commandment of the Lord is pure, enlightening the eyes. The fear of the Lord is clean, enduring forever; the judgments of the Lord are true; they are righteous altogether. They are more desirable than gold, yes, than much fine gold; sweeter also than honey and the drippings of the honeycomb. Moreover, by them Thy servant is warned; in keeping them there is great reward.

And again in Psalm 119:97–104,

> O how I love Thy law! It is my meditation all the day. Thy commandments make me wiser than my enemies, for they are ever mine. I have more insight than all my teachers, for Thy testimonies are my meditation. I understand more than the aged, because I have observed Thy precepts. I have restrained my feet from every evil way, that I may keep Thy word. I have not turned aside from Thine ordinances, for Thou Thyself hast taught me. How sweet are Thy words to my taste! Yes, sweeter than honey to my mouth! From Thy pre-

cepts I get understanding; therefore I hate every false way.

In both passages David is saying that the joy in his life is directly linked to his understanding and application of God's Word. To enjoy your Bible, you must use it!

Every truth God reveals in His Word must be obeyed and put into action, or our knowledge will leave us with a theology as clear as ice and twice as cold. Application of God's Word completes the Bible-study process.

Irving Jensen illustrates this principle the following way.[1] Let this circle represent the Bible:

God desires His Word to be at the center of our lives, instructing, motivating, and empowering us. Around this circle let's put a larger circle that represents your life:

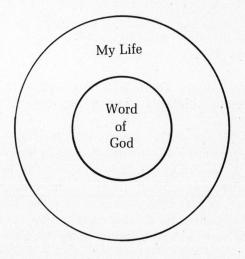

With the Word central in your life, it will convict you of sin (Hebrews 4:12, 13). It will cleanse and purify you (John 15:3; 17:17). It will equip you for battle (Ephesians 6:17). It will give you counsel for wisdom (Psalm 119:24). It will change your life. And as it changes your life, it will work through you to change the world.

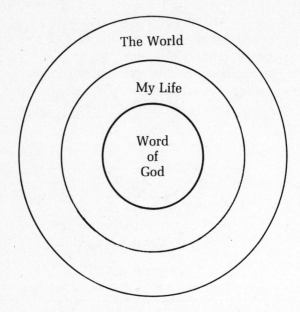

This is God's desire. Through His Word, He wants to change you and thereby ultimately affect the world. (Matthew 28:19, 20).

Jack Eckerd, founder of the Eckerd drugstore chain, is a prime example of how one life transformed by the Word of God can affect the world. Chuck Colson, a friend of Jack Eckerd, tells how after he committed his life to Christ, Eckerd walked through one of his drugstores and saw the *Playboy* and *Penthouse* magazines on its shelves with new eyes. If Christ was going to have the final authority in his life, then the pornographic literature would have to be removed from his stores. Though retired at the time, he called his president and insisted the magazines be removed. In spite of the fact that he and the chain stood to lose substantial profits, *Playboy* and *Penthouse* were removed from the 1,700 Eckerd drugstores.

Later, when Jack Eckerd was asked by Chuck Colson why he had removed the magazines, he answered simply, "God wouldn't let me off the hook."[2] He had to obey His Word.

A study of Christ's life will reveal that Jesus expected His followers to apply His Word. He commanded those who heard it to act in accordance to it. He called men to preach, watch, pray, come, follow, go and do likewise, sell, go and tell. Similar expectations pervade the Scriptures. James 1:22 adds, "Prove yourselves doers of the word, and not merely hearers who delude themselves."

Knowing God's Word is not enough; it needs to be worked out in your life. As Howard Hendricks suggests, "to know and not to do is not to know at all." Only those who do God's Word know it in the biblical sense.

Fortunately, God has not left us alone in applying His Word. In 1 Corinthians 2:14 we are told that the role of the Holy Spirit is to change the heart of the interpreter so that he accepts the message that is conveyed. Without the Holy Spirit, man does not have the ability to see the worth or value of biblical teachings. A person could actually read and study the Bible for many years and yet fail to see its intended meaning without the Holy Spirit.

Martin Luther said, "The Bible cannot be understood simply by study or talent; you must count only on the influence of the Holy Spirit."

John Calvin wrote, "The testimony of the Spirit is superior to reason. These words will not obtain full credit in the hearts of men until they are sealed by the inward testimony of the Spirit."

Or, as another suggested, without the Holy Spirit man will

"gnaw the bark of Scripture without getting to the wood."

Your ultimate hope for understanding what the Bible means by what it says is found through a personal relationship with Jesus Christ. If you have believed in Christ and received Him as your personal Savior, then you have received the Holy Spirit (Romans 8:9). Through the Spirit, God gives you the ability to see the meaning and application of the Word.

J. I. Packer says, "Those who would live under the authority of the Spirit must bow before the Word as the Spirit's textbook, while those who live under the authority of Scripture must seek the Spirit as its interpreter."[3]

The Christian walk is not an either/or proposition. It's both/and. Both God and you. It requires your 100 percent and God's 100 percent. Fortunately, as Tim Timmons says, "God's 100 percent makes your 100 percent possible." Practically, you must give 100 percent of yourself to God as you give 100 percent to studying His Word. As you do that, His Word will come alive and transform your life through the work of the Holy Spirit.

Charles Swindoll relates the story of Ignace Jan Paderewski, the famous composer-pianist, who was scheduled to perform at a great concert hall in America.

> It was an evening to remember—black tuxedos and long evening dresses—a high-society extravaganza.
> Present in the audience that evening was a mother with her fidgety nine-year-old son. As she turned to talk with friends, her son could stay seated no longer. He slipped away from her side, strangely drawn to the ebony concert grand Steinway and its leather-tufted stool on the huge stage flooded with blinding lights. Without much notice from the sophisticated audience, the boy sat down at the stool, staring wide-eyed at the black and white keys. He placed his small, trembling fingers in the right location and began to play "Chopsticks."

The roar of the crowd was hushed as hundreds of frowning faces turned in his direction. Irritated and embarrassed, they began to shout: "Get that boy away from there!" "Who'd bring a kid that young in here?" "Where's his mother?" "Somebody stop him!"

Backstage, the master overheard the sounds out front. Hurriedly, he grabbed his coat and rushed toward the stage. Without one word of announcement, he stooped over behind the boy, reached around both sides, and began to improvise a countermelody to harmonize with and enhance "Chopsticks." As the two of them played together, Paderewski kept whispering in the boy's ear, "Keep going. Don't quit, son. Keep on playing . . . don't stop . . . don't quit."[4]

As you read and study God's Word, depend on God's Spirit. Humbly ask God to teach you and lead you. Make it your goal each time you study the Bible to realize its intended meaning in your life. Rote learning is not enough. God never intended you to hide His Word in your notebook. He wants it to change your life, and He has given the Holy Spirit to you to ensure this will happen. He wants you to experience the joy that stems from the application of His Word to your life.

Are you enjoying your Bible yet? God has made it possible for you to experience many years of enjoyment through His Word. It's possible, through your personal diligent study and the power of the Holy Spirit who is yours in Christ.

On June 16, 1977, Ford Motor Company began its seventy-fifth year. A few days later, Henry Ford II, grandson of Henry Ford, penned these words:

When my grandfather founded Ford Motor Company on June 16, 1903, he had a primary purpose in mind. As a farm boy he knew from firsthand experience that farming could be backbreaking work and he knew that machinery could ease the burden. He saw the automobile as a piece of machinery. He envisioned the car, not as a luxury vehicle for the rich, but as a means for the average man to make his life—and his family's—easier and happier. It soon became apparent that the car not only would ease man's burden, but that it would enable him to enjoy a fuller life.[5]

The automobile has become such a vital part of our lives today that most of us can't imagine what life would be like without it. However, the joy a car can bring to men is miniscule in comparison to the impact of God's Word. It's there for the taking, but first you must get in, get started, and get on your way. If you'll do that, God promises a richer, fuller, more meaningful life as you venture on in your study of God's Word.

TUNE-UP 25

Using 2 Timothy 2:15, make:

1. Two observations
   A. _____
   B. _____
2. A concise interpretation _____

   _____
3. A final application _____

   _____

NOTES

1. Irving L. Jensen, *Enjoying Your Bible* (Chicago: Moody Press, 1969), 116–118.
2. Charles Colson, *Who Speaks for God?* (Westchester: Crossway Books, 1985), 60–61.

3. J. I. Packer, *Keep in Step With the Spirit* (Old Tappan: Fleming H. Revell Co., 1984), 240.
4. Charles R. Swindoll, *Growing Strong in the Seasons of Life* (Portland: Multnomah Press, 1983), 48–49.
5. *1978 Ford Fairmont Owner's Guide* (Canada: Ford Motor Co., 1978), 1.

NINE

MAINTENANCE SCHEDULES

In this section I will give you several suggestions you might find helpful. Some of these suggestions will be specifically applicable to Bible reading alone, while others will apply to both Bible reading and Bible study. My intention is to assist you in getting both started. If you have not formulated a plan by now, I encourage you to adopt one of these or write your own. My hope and prayer is that you will find a method that is right for you and that you will *get started today!*

If you have never read the Bible before, you might try reading the Old Testament in the following order.[1]

Genesis: History of the Creation, Fall, and Covenant in patriarchal history.

Exodus: History of Israel's liberation and formation as the people of God.

Joshua: History of the military conquest of the promised land.

Judges: History of the transition from a tribal federation to a monarchy.

First Samuel: History of the emerging monarchy, with Samuel, Saul, and David.

Second Samuel: The reign of David, the golden age of Israel.

First Kings: History of Solomon and the division of the kingdom.

Second Kings: History of the fall of Israel and the beginnings of the prophets.

Ezra: History of the return from exile.

Nehemiah: History of restoration of Jerusalem.

Amos and Hosea: Examples of minor prophets.

Jeremiah: Example of major prophets.

Ecclesiastes and Song of Solomon: Examples of wisdom literature.

Psalms and Proverbs: Examples of Hebrew poetry.

Here is a similar list that will get you off to a good start in the New Testament.

Luke: Life and teaching of Jesus.
Acts: History of the early church.
Ephesians: Introduction to teaching of Paul.
First Corinthians: Teaching in the life of the church.
First Peter: Introduction to Peter.
First Timothy: Introduction to pastoral epistles.
Hebrews: Theology of Christ.
Romans: Paul's theology.

Here is another suggestion you might find helpful. If you follow this schedule, you will read the entire Bible in three years.[2]

	First Year	Second Year	Third Year
Jan.	Mark	Psalms 42–72	I and II Kings
		Romans & Hebrews	
Feb.	Genesis	Ecclesiastes	Psalms 107—150
Mar.		Numbers	Jeremiah–Lamentations
Apr.	Acts	Job	Ezra–Nehemiah–Esther
			Song of Solomon
May	Exodus	Galatians to Colossians	I and II Chronicles
June		Deuteronomy	Hosea to Malachi
Jul.	Psalms 1–41	I Peter to III John	James, Jude, Philemon
Aug.	Matthew	Psalms 73–106	Isaiah
Sep.	Leviticus	John	
Oct.	Proverbs	Joshua	I Tim.–Titus–II Tim.
		Judges–Ruth	
Nov.	Ezekiel–Daniel	Corinthians–Thessalonians	Luke
Dec.	Revelation	I and II Samuel	

For maximum absorption of your Bible try rereading a specific number of chapters over a period of thirty days. Here is a plan that will take you through the New Testament in thirty months.[3]

Month	Reading
1	1, 2, 3 John
2	John 1–7
3	John 8–14
4	John 15–21
5	1 Corinthians 1–8
6	1 Corinthians 9–16
7	2 Corinthians

8	Matthew 1–9
9	Matthew 10–18
10	Matthew 19–28
11	Galatians/Ephesians
12	Philippians/Colossians
13	Mark 1–8
14	Mark 9–16
15	1 & 2 Thessalonians
16	1 & 2 Timothy
17	Luke 1–8
18	Luke 9–16
19	Luke 17–24
20	Titus/Philemon/Jude
21	Hebrews
22	James
23	Acts 1–9
24	Acts 10–18
25	Acts 19–28
26	Romans 1–8
27	Romans 9–16
28	1 & 2 Peter
29	Revelation 1–11
30	Revelation 12–22

You may be interested in doing a study on prayer. Here is a list that will take you through the major prayers in the Bible.[4]

Old Testament Prayers

Aaron and the Priests	Numbers 6:22–26	Blessing for Israel
Abraham	Genesis 15:2	For a son
Abraham	Genesis 17:17	For Ishmael's acceptance
Abraham's servant	Genesis 24:12	Success in his mission
Agur	Proverbs 30:1	For moderation
Asa	II Chronicles 14:11	When entering battle
Daniel	Daniel 9:4–19	For restoration
David	II Samuel 7:18	To spare the nation
David	Psalm 51	For restoration
David	II Samuel 24:17	To spare the nation

David	I Chronicles 29:10	Thanksgiving
Elijah	I Kings 17:20	For restoration of life
Elijah	I Kings 18:36,37	For vindication
Elijah	I Kings 19:4	For release from life
Elisha	II Kings 6:17	For vision
Ezekiel	Ezekiel 9:8	Intercession for the people
Ezra	Ezra 9:5–15	Confession for the people
Habakkuk	Habakkuk 2:1–20	For revival
Hannah	I Samuel 1:11	For a son
Hezekiah	II Kings 19:15	For protection
Hezekiah	II Chronicles 3:18	For healing
Hezekiah	II Chronicles 30:18	For pardon for his people
Israel	Deuteronomy 21:6–8	For forgiveness
Israel	Deuteronomy 26:5–10	Expiation for murder
Israel	Deuteronomy 26:13–15	For tithing
Jabez	I Chronicles 4:10	For divine blessing
Jacob	Genesis 32:9	For deliverance
Jehoshaphat	II Chronicles 20:6	For protection
Jeremiah	Jeremiah 14:7–9	For salvation
Jeremiah	Jeremiah 15:15–18	For comfort
Jonah	Jonah 2:2	For deliverance
Joshua	Joshua 7:7–9	Cry of distress
Levites	Nehemiah 9:5	Adoration
Manoah	Judges 13:8,9	For divine guidance
Moses	Exodus 32:11–14	For forgiveness
Moses	Numbers 10:35	For protection
Moses	Numbers 11:11–15	For help to govern
Moses	Numbers 12:13	For healing
Moses	Numbers 14:13–19	For vindication
Moses	Numbers 27:15	For a successor
Moses	Deuteronomy 3:24	For entrance to the land
Nehemiah	Nehemiah 1:5–11	Confession and rebuilding
Nehemiah	Nehemiah 4:4,5	For protection
Samson	Judges 16:28	For avenging
Solomon	I Kings 3:5–9	For wisdom to govern
Solomon	I Kings 8:22–53	Dedication of the temple

New Testament Prayers

Jesus	Luke 22:39–46	For courage
Jesus	Luke 23:34	For forgiveness

Jesus	John 17:1–26	For safekeeping
Disciples	Matthew 6:9–15	The divinely given pattern
Disciples	Luke 11:2–4	for prayer
Disciples	Acts 4:23–31	For boldness
Paul	Romans 1:9–12	For opportunity
Paul	Ephesians 1:16–23	For knowledge and power
Paul	Ephesians 3:14–21	For knowledge
Paul	Philippians 1:8–11	For maturity
Paul	Colossians 1:9–14	For fruitfulness

Studying the parables of Christ has been one of my favorite ways to get into the Bible. Below is a study I did. I found it helpful to categorize them under the following thirteen headings:

I. **The people of the kingdom**
—The Parable of the Soils
Matthew 13:1–9, 18–23;
Mark 4:1–9, 13–20
Luke 8:4–8, 11–15

II. **The conflict of the kingdom**
—The Parable of the Weeds
Matthew 13:24–30, 36–43

III. **The growth of the kingdom**
—The Parable of the Mustard Seed
Matthew 13:31, 32
Mark 4:30–32
Luke 13:18, 19
—The Parable of the Leaven
Matthew 13:33; Luke 13:20–21

IV. **The value of the kingdom**
—The Parable of the Hidden Treasure
Matthew 13:44
—The Parable of the Costly Pearl
Matthew 13:45, 46

V. **The invitation of the kingdom**
—The Parable of the Royal Feast
Matthew 22:1–14
Luke 14:15–24

VI. **The grace of the kingdom**
—The Parable of the Lost Sheep
   Luke 15:4–7
—The Parable of the Lost Coin
   Luke 15:8–10
—The Parable of the Lost Son
   Luke 15:11–32
—The Parable of the Gracious Employer
   Matthew 19:30–20:16

VII. **The forgiveness of the kingdom**
—The Parable of the Unforgiving Servant
   Matthew 18:21–35

VIII. **The love of the kingdom**
—The Parable of the Loving Samaritan
   Luke 10:25–37

IX. **The stewardship of the kingdom**
—The Parable of the Foresighted Steward
   Luke 16:1–13
—The Parable of the Talents
   Matthew 25:14–20
—The Parable of the Pounds
   Luke 19:11–27

X. **Our conduct in the kingdom**
—The Parable of the Friends at Midnight
   Luke 11:5–13
—The Parable of the Unjust Judge
   Luke 18:1–8

XI. **The rejection of the kingdom**
—The Parable About Two Sons
   Matthew 21:28–30
—The Parable About One Son
   Matthew 21:33–46

> Mark 12:1–12
> Luke 20:9–19

XII. The consummation of the kingdom
—The Parable About Sleepy Saints
> Matthew 25:1–13

XIII. The judgment of the kingdom
—The Parable of the Dragnet
> Matthew 13:47–51
—The Parable of the Rich Man and Lazarus
> Luke 16:19–31

A study of key characters in the Bible will bring the Bible alive.

Get your concordance out and see what you can learn about the following forty-five characters. I have listed them in the chronological order in which they occur in the Bible.

1.	God	20.	Saul
2.	Adam	21.	David
3.	Eve	22.	Solomon
4.	Satan	23.	Rehoboam
5.	Noah	24.	Asa
6.	Abraham	25.	Elijah
7.	Isaac	26.	Elisha
8.	Jacob	27.	Jonah
9.	Joseph	28.	Isaiah
10.	Moses	29.	Jeremiah
11.	Aaron	30.	Daniel
12.	Pharaoh	31.	Zerubbabel
13.	Joshua	32.	Esther
14.	Caleb	33.	Ezra
15.	Deborah	34.	Nehemiah
16.	Gideon	35.	John the Baptist
17.	Samson	36.	Jesus Christ
18.	Ruth	37.	Simon Peter
19.	Samuel	38.	James

39. John
40. Stephen
41. Philip
42. Barnabas

43. Paul
44. James, Jesus' brother
45. Timothy

An excellent way to understand the historical flow of the Old Testament is through a key-chapter study. Here are sixteen key chapters and books to study.

1. The creation account—Genesis 1–2
2. The fall of man—Genesis 3
3. The flood—Genesis 6–9
4. The tower of Babel—Genesis 11
5. The call of Abraham—Genesis 12
6. The move of Egypt—Genesis 46, 47
7. The exodus from Egypt—Exodus 7–12
8. The Passover—Exodus 12
9. The law at Mount Sinai—Exodus 19–24
10. The wilderness wanderings—Numbers 13–14
11. The return to Israel—Joshua 11
12. The period of the judges—Judges
13. The united kingdom, 1 Samuel 9:27; 10:1; 2 Samuel 5:4, 5; 1 Kings 10:6–8
14. The divided kingdom, 1 Kings 12:26–33
15. The captivities, 2 Kings 17, 25
16. The Israelites return, Ezra

Here are a few short New Testament passages you may want to study.[5]

Overcoming worry—Matthew 6:25–34
Being ready for the end—Matthew 24:36–51
The Great Commission—Matthew 28:16–20
The parable of the sower—Mark 4:1–20
Prayer—Luke 11:1–13
The cost of discipleship—Luke 14:25–35
Jesus, the Word of God—John 1:1–18

The vine and the branches—John 15:1–17
The world's wickedness—Romans 1:18–32
Righteousness through faith—Romans 3:21–26
Peace with God through Christ—Romans 5:1–11
Death to sin—Romans 6:1–14
The Spirit's control—Romans 8:5–11
Honoring God with our bodies—1 Corinthians 6:12–20
Love—1 Corinthians 13:1–13
Our ministry—2 Corinthians 5:11–21
Freedom in the Spirit—Galatians 5:13–26
Spiritual unity—Ephesians 6:10–18
Humility—Philippians 2:1–11
Christ above all—Colossians 1:15–20
Christ's second coming—1 Thessalonians 4:13–5:11
Work—2 Thessalonians 3:6–13
Perseverance—Hebrews 10:19–39
God's discipline—Hebrews 12:1–13
Faith and deeds—James 2:14–26
Hope—1 Peter 1:3–9
Wives and husbands—1 Peter 3:1–7
Loving others—1 John 3:16–24
New Jerusalem—Revelation 21:1–8

After you purchase a few resource books, you may want to try a word study. Here is a selected list of key Bible words to study.

atonement	kingdom	Passover
baptism	gospel	sacrifice
faith	spirit	disciple
holiness	heaven	fellowship
love	hell	redemption
conscience	obedience	rapture
rewards	fear	covenant
Satan	awe	marriage
judgment	omnipotence	divorce
repentance	temptation	counsel
mercy	humility	trust
forgiveness	joy	tithe

preach	inspiration	evangelist
peace	eternal	antichrist
worry	law	sabbath
hope	election	church

Are you interested in reading the entire Bible through in one year? Here's an excellent guide that will give you a daily schedule. Just be sure to keep from getting behind.[6]

Date	JANUARY MORNING MATT.	EVENING GEN.	Date	FEBRUARY MORNING MATT.	EVENING EX.
1	1	1, 2, 3	1	21: 1–22	27, 28
2	2	4, 5, 6	2	21:23–46	29, 30
3	3	7, 8, 9	3	22: 1–22	31, 32, 33
4	4	10, 11, 12	4	22:23–46	34, 35
5	5: 1–26	13, 14, 15	5	23: 1–22	36, 37, 38
6	5:27–48	16, 17	6	23:23–39	39, 40
7	6: 1–18	18, 19			**LEV.**
8	6:19–34	20, 21, 22	7	24: 1–28	1, 2, 3
9	7	23, 24	8	24:29–51	4, 5
10	8: 1–17	25, 26	9	25: 1–30	6, 7
11	8:18–34	27, 28	10	25:31–46	8, 9, 10
12	9: 1–17	29, 30	11	26: 1–25	11, 12
13	9:18–38	31, 32	12	26:26–50	13
14	10: 1–20	33, 34, 35	13	26:51–75	14
15	10:21–42	36, 37, 38	14	27: 1–26	15, 16
16	11	39, 40	15	27:27–50	17, 18
17	12: 1–23	41, 42	16	27:51–66	19, 20
18	12:24–50	43, 44, 45	17	28	21, 22
19	13: 1–30	46, 47, 48		**MARK**	
20	13:31–58	49, 50	18	1: 1–22	23, 24
		EX.	19	1:23–45	25
21	14: 1–21	1, 2, 3	20	2	26, 27
22	14:22–36	4, 5, 6			**NUM.**
23	15: 1–20	7, 8	21	3: 1–19	1, 2
24	15:21–39	9, 10, 11	22	3:20–35	3, 4
25	16	12, 13	23	4: 1–20	5, 6
26	17	14, 15	24	4:21–41	7, 8
27	18: 1–20	16, 17, 18	25	5: 1–20	9, 10, 11
28	18:21–35	19, 20	26	5:21–43	12, 13, 14
29	19	21, 22	27	6: 1–29	15, 16
30	20: 1–16	23, 24	28	6:30–56	17, 18, 19
31	20:17–34	25, 26	29	7: 1–13	20, 21, 22

	MARCH				**APRIL**	
Date	**MORNING** **MARK**	**EVENING** **NUM.**		**Date**	**MORNING** **LUKE**	**EVENING** **JUDG.**
1	7:14–37	23, 24, 25		1	6:27–49	13, 14, 15
2	8: 1–21	26, 27		2	7: 1–30	16, 17, 18
3	8:22–38	28, 29, 30		3	7:31–50	19, 20, 21
4	9: 1–29	31, 32, 33				**RUTH**
5	9:30–50	34, 35, 36		4	8: 1–25	1, 2, 3, 4
		DEUT.				**1 SAM.**
6	10: 1–31	1, 2		5	8:26–56	1, 2, 3
7	10:32–52	3, 4		6	9: 1–17	4, 5, 6
8	11: 1–18	5, 6, 7		7	9:18–36	7, 8, 9
9	11:19–33	8, 9, 10		8	9:37–62	10, 11, 12
10	12: 1–27	11, 12, 13		9	10: 1–24	13, 14
11	12:28–44	14, 15, 16		10	10:25–42	15, 16
12	13: 1–20	17, 18, 19		11	11: 1–28	17, 18
13	13:21–37	20, 21, 22		12	11:29–54	19, 20, 21
14	14: 1–26	23, 24, 25		13	12: 1–31	22, 23, 24
15	14:27–53	26, 27		14	12:32–59	25, 26
16	14:54–72	28, 29		15	13: 1–22	27, 28, 29
17	15: 1–25	30, 31		16	13:23–35	30, 31
18	15:26–47	32, 33, 34				**2 SAM.**
		JOSH.		17	14: 1–24	1, 2
19	16	1, 2, 3		18	14:25–35	3, 4, 5
	LUKE			19	15: 1–10	6, 7, 8
20	1: 1–20	4, 5, 6		20	15:11–32	9, 10, 11
21	1:21–38	7, 8, 9		21	16	12, 13
22	1:39–56	10, 11, 12		22	17: 1–19	14, 15
23	1:57–80	13, 14, 15		23	17:20–37	16, 17, 18
24	2: 1–24	16, 17, 18		24	18: 1–23	19, 20
25	2:25–52	19, 20, 21		25	18:24–43	21, 22
26	3	22, 23, 24		26	19: 1–27	23, 24
		JUDG.				**1 KIN.**
27	4: 1–30	1, 2, 3		27	19:28–48	1, 2
28	4:31–44	4, 5, 6		28	20: 1–26	3, 4, 5
29	5: 1–16	7, 8		29	20:27–47	6, 7
30	5:17–39	9, 10		30	21: 1–19	8, 9
31	6: 1–26	11, 12				

	MAY			JUNE	
Date	**MORNING**	**EVENING**	**Date**	**MORNING**	**EVENING**
	LUKE	**1 KIN.**		**JOHN**	**2 CHR.**
1	21:20–38	10, 11	1	12:27–50	15, 16
2	22: 1–20	12, 13	2	13: 1–20	17, 18
3	22:21–46	14, 15	3	13:21–38	19, 20
4	22:47–71	16, 17, 18	4	14	21, 22
5	23: 1–25	19, 20	5	15	23, 24
6	23:26–56	21, 22	6	16	25, 26, 27
		2 KIN.	7	17	28, 29
7	24: 1–35	1, 2, 3	8	18: 1–18	30, 31
8	24:36–53	4, 5, 6	9	18:19–40	32, 33
	JOHN		10	19: 1–22	34, 35, 36
9	1: 1–28	7, 8, 9			**EZRA**
10	1:29–51	10, 11, 12	11	19:23–42	1, 2
11	2	13, 14	12	20	3, 4, 5
12	3: 1–18	15, 16	13	21	6, 7, 8
13	3:19–38	17, 18		**ACTS**	
14	4: 1–30	19, 20, 21	14	1	9, 10
15	4:31–54	22, 23			**NEH.**
16	5: 1–24	24, 25	15	2: 1–21	1, 2, 3
		1 CHR.	16	2:22–47	4, 5, 6
17	5:25–47	1, 2, 3	17	3	7, 8, 9
18	6: 1–21	4, 5, 6	18	4: 1–22	10, 11
19	6:22–44	7, 8, 9	19	4:23–37	12, 13
20	6:45–71	10, 11, 12			**ESTH.**
21	7: 1–27	13, 14, 15	20	5: 1–21	1, 2
22	7:28–53	16, 17, 18	21	5:22–42	3, 4, 5
23	8: 1–27	19, 20, 21	22	6	6, 7, 8
24	8:28–59	22, 23, 24	23	7: 1–21	9, 10
25	9: 1–23	25, 26, 27			**JOB**
26	9:24–41	28, 29	24	7:22–43	1, 2
		2 CHR.	25	7:44–60	3, 4
27	10: 1–23	1, 2, 3	26	8: 1–25	5, 6, 7
28	10:24–42	4, 5, 6	27	8:26–40	8, 9, 10
29	11: 1–29	7, 8, 9	28	9: 1–21	11, 12, 13
30	11:30–57	10, 11, 12	29	9:22–43	14, 15, 16
31	12: 1–26	13, 14	30	10: 1–23	17, 18, 19

	JULY			**AUGUST**	
Date	MORNING ACTS	EVENING JOB	Date	MORNING ROM.	EVENING PS.
1	10:24–48	20, 21	1	4	57, 58, 59
2	11	22, 23, 24	2	5	60, 61, 62
3	12	25, 26, 27	3	6	63, 64, 65
4	13: 1–25	28, 29	4	7	66, 67
5	13:26–52	30, 31	5	8: 1–21	68, 69
6	14	32, 33	6	8:22–39	70, 71
7	15: 1–21	34, 35	7	9: 1–15	72, 73
8	15:22–41	36, 37	8	9:16–33	74, 75, 76
9	16: 1–21	38, 39, 40	9	10	77, 78
10	16:22–40	41, 42	10	11: 1–18	79, 80
		PS.	11	11:19–36	81, 82, 83
11	17: 1–15	1, 2, 3	12	12	84, 85, 86
12	17:16–34	4, 5, 6	13	13	87, 88
13	18	7, 8, 9	14	14	89, 90
14	19: 1–20	10, 11, 12	15	15: 1–13	91, 92, 93
15	19:21–41	13, 14, 15	16	15:14–33	94, 95, 96
16	20: 1–16	16, 17	17	16	97, 98, 99
17	20:17–38	18, 19		**1 COR.**	
18	21: 1–17	20, 21, 22	18	1	100, 101, 102
19	21:18–40	23, 24, 25	19	2	103, 104
20	22	26, 27, 28	20	3	105, 106
21	23: 1–15	29, 30	21	4	107, 108, 109
22	23:16–35	31, 32	22	5	110, 111, 112
23	24	33, 34	23	6	113, 114, 115
24	25	35, 36	24	7: 1–19	116, 117, 118
25	26	37, 38, 39	25	7:20–40	119: 1–88
26	27: 1–26	40, 41, 42	26	8	119: 89–176
27	27:27–44	43, 44, 45	27	9	120, 121, 122
28	28	46, 47, 48	28	10: 1–18	123, 124, 125
	ROM.		29	10:19–33	126, 127, 128
29	1	49, 50	30	11: 1–16	129, 130, 131
30	2	51, 52, 53	31	11:17–34	132, 133, 134
31	3	54, 55, 56			

	SEPTEMBER			**OCTOBER**	
Date	MORNING	EVENING	Date	MORNING	EVENING
	1 COR.	**PS.**		**EPH.**	**IS.**
1	12	135, 136	1	4	11, 12 13
2	13	137, 138, 139	2	5: 1–16	14, 15, 16
3	14: 1–20	140, 141, 142	3	5:17–33	17, 18, 19
4	14:21–40	143, 144, 145	4	6	20, 21, 22
5	15: 1–28	146, 147,		**PHIL.**	
6	15:29–58	148, 149, 150	5	1	23, 24, 25
		PROV.	6	2	26, 27
7	16	1, 2	7	3	28, 29
	2 COR.		8	4	30, 31
8	1	3, 4, 5		**COL.**	
9	2	6, 7	9	1	32, 33
10	3	8, 9	10	2	34, 35, 36
11	4	10, 11, 12	11	3	37, 38
12	5	13, 14, 15	12	4	39, 40
13	6	16, 17, 18		**1 THESS.**	
14	7	19, 20, 21	13	1	41, 42
15	8	22, 23, 24	14	2	43, 44
16	9	25, 26	15	3	45, 46
17	10	27, 28, 29	16	4	47, 48, 49
18	11: 1–15	30, 31	17	5	50, 51, 52
		ECCL.		**2 THESS.**	
19	11:16–33	1, 2, 3	18	1	53, 54, 55
20	12	4, 5, 6	19	2	56, 57, 58
21	13	7, 8, 9	20	3	59, 60, 61
	GAL.			**1 TIM.**	
22	1	10, 11, 12	21	1	62, 63, 64
		SONG	22	2	65, 66
23	2	1, 2, 3			**JER.**
24	3	4, 5	23	3	1, 2
25	4	6, 7, 8	24	4	3, 4, 5
		IS.	25	5	6, 7, 8
26	5	1, 2	26	6	9, 10, 11
27	6	3, 4		**2 TIM.**	
	EPH.		27	1	12, 13, 14
28	1	5, 6	28	2	15, 16, 17
29	2	7, 8	29	3	18, 19
30	3	9, 10	30	4	20, 21
				TITUS	
			31	1	22, 23

	NOVEMBER				**DECEMBER**	
Date	**MORNING**	**EVENING**		**Date**	**MORNING**	**EVENING**
	TITUS	**JER.**			**2 PET.**	**EZEK.**
1	2	24, 25, 26		1	3	40, 41
2	3	27, 28, 29			**1 JOHN**	
3	**PHILEM.**	30, 31		2	1	42, 43, 44
	HEB.			3	2	45, 46
4	1	32, 33		4	3	47, 48
5	2	34, 35, 36				**DAN.**
6	3	37, 38, 39		5	4	1, 2
7	4	40, 41, 42		6	5	3, 4
8	5	43, 44, 45		7	**2 JOHN**	5, 6, 7
9	6	46, 47		8	**3 JOHN**	8, 9, 10
10	7	48, 49		9	**JUDE**	11, 12
11	8	50			**REV.**	**HOS.**
12	9	51, 52		10	1	1, 2, 3, 4
		LAM.		11	2	5, 6, 7, 8
13	10: 1–18	1, 2		12	3	9, 10, 11
14	10:19–39	3, 4, 5		13	4	12, 13, 14
		EZEK.		14	5	**JOEL**
15	11: 1–19	1, 2				**AMOS**
16	11:20–40	3, 4		15	6	1, 2, 3
17	12	5, 6, 7		16	7	4, 5, 6
18	13	8, 9, 10		17	8	7, 8, 9
	JAMES			18	9	**OBAD.**
19	1	11, 12, 13		19	10	**JON.**
20	2	14, 15				**MIC.**
21	3	16, 17		20	11	1, 2, 3
22	4	18, 19		21	12	4, 5
23	5	20, 21		22	13	6, 7
	1 PET.			23	14	**NAH.**
24	1	22, 23		24	15	**HAB.**
25	2	24, 25, 26		25	16	**ZEPH.**
26	3	27, 28, 29		26	17	**HAG.**
27	4	30, 31, 32				**ZECH.**
28	5	33, 34		27	18	1, 2, 3, 4
	2 PET.			28	19	5, 6, 7, 8
29	1	35, 36		29	20	9, 10, 11, 12
30	2	37, 38, 39		30	21	13, 14
				31	22	**MAL.**

NOTES

1. R. C. Sproul. *Knowing Scripture.* (Downers Grove: InterVarsity Press, 1977), 122, 123.

2. Irving L. Jensen. *Enjoying Your Bible.* (Chicago: Moody Press, 1969), 127.

3. John MacArthur. "Thru the New Testament in Thirty Months" (Sun Valley: Grace Community Church, 1981).

4. Lloyd M. Perry and Walden Howard. *How to Study the Bible.* (Old Tappan: Fleming H. Revell Co., 1957), 133–135.

5. Rick Yohn. *First Hand Joy.* (Colorado Springs: Navpress, 1982), 61, 62.

6. *New American Standard Bible.* (Nashville: Thomas Nelson Publishers, 1985), 26, 27.

SPECIFICATIONS
Answers to
Tune-ups

TUNE-UP #1

1. A. Communication B. Authority C. Reliability
2. Psalm 19:7 = Reliability
   2 Peter 1:20, 21 = Authority
   Jeremiah 15:16 = Communication
3. Hebrew, Aramaic
4. Greek

TUNE-UP #2

"Truly, truly, I say to you, he who hears My Word, and believes Him who sent Me, has eternal life, and does not come into judgment, but has passed out of death into life."

113

TUNE-UP #3

1. Genesis, Exodus, Leviticus, Numbers, Deuteronomy
2. Joshua, Judges, Ruth, 1 and 2 Samuel, 1 and 2 Kings, 1 and 2 Chronicles, Ezra, Nehemiah, Esther
3. Job, Psalms, Proverbs, Ecclessiastes, Song of Solomon
4. Isaiah, Jeremiah, Lamentations, Ezekiel, Daniel, Hosea, Joel, Amos, Obadiah, Jonah, Micah, Nahum, Habakkuk, Zephaniah, Haggai, Zechariah, Malachi
5. 39

TUNE-UP #4

4 — Conquest Stage
8 — Captivity Stage
2 — Patriarchal Stage
6 — United Kingdom
3 — Exodus Stage
9 — Return Stage
5 — Judges Stage
1 — Creation Stage
7 — Chaotic Kingdom Stage

TUNE-UP #5

1. Matthew, Mark, Luke, John, Acts
2. Romans, 1 and 2 Corinthians, Galatians, Ephesians, Philippians, Colossians, 1 and 2 Thessalonians, 1 and 2 Timothy, Titus, Philemon, Hebrews, James, 1 and 2 Peter, 1–3 John, Jude
3. Revelation
4. 27

TUNE-UP #6

1. Exegesis   2. Eisegesis

TUNE-UP #7

Prose = Matthew 4:18
Poetry = Psalm 46:7
Prophecy = John 2:18, 19

TUNE-UP #8

"If then you have been raised up with Christ, keep seeking the things above, where Christ is, seated at the right hand of God. (Set your mind on) the things above, (not on) the things that are on earth. For you have died and your life is hidden with Christ in God. When Christ, who is our life, is revealed, then you also will be revealed with Him in glory. Therefore consider the members of your earthly body as dead to [immorality, impurity, passion, evil desire, and greed, which amounts to idolatry.] For it is on account of these things that the wrath of God will come, and (in them you also once walked), when you were living in them."

TUNE-UP #9

Husbands / love / your wives.
Wives / be subject / to your husbands.
Children / obey / your parents.

TUNE-UP #10

• Peter, John, lame beggar
• The lame beggar was healed
• Walking, leaping, praising God

- At the temple gate—Beautiful
- The ninth hour (3:00 P.M.)
- In the power of Jesus' name

TUNE-UP #11

1. Love is permanent, in contrast with prophecies, tongues, and knowledge—all of which one day will cease to exist.
2. Without love, gifts are nothing. Gifts must be exercised in the context of fervent Christian love.
3. Love is outgoing, long-suffering, self-giving, self-effacing—it is the key ingredient that will resolve the problems at Corinth.
4. The commandments are fulfilled through love of God and love of man. These two are the crux of new life in Christ.

TUNE-UP #12

Contextually, love is equated with *patience, kindness, truth, forbearance, belief, hope, endurance.*

Contextually, love is contrasted with *jealousy, bragging, arrogance, acting unbecomingly, seeking one's own, being provoked, taking credit for wrongs suffered, rejoicing in unrighteousness.*

Grammatically, love is a *noun.* By definition, love is a *verb.* That is indicated by *the descriptive verbs of action.*

Syntactically, *love is the focal point of the passage. It alone stands as supreme in comparison to all else.*

TUNE-UP #13

1 Corinthians 2:1; 3:2—Paul had, previous to the writing of 1 Corinthians, personally visited the Corinthians.

1 Corinthians 5:9—After Paul's visit, he wrote the Corinthians a letter. It is possible this letter was lost.

1 Corinthians 1:11–13—There were divisions in the church.

1 Corinthians 7:1, 25—The Corinthians had written Paul a letter asking him for advice on marriage.

1 Corinthians 8:1–4—The Corinthians had written Paul and asked him about whether or not it was permissible to eat meat that had previously been given to idols.

1 Corinthians 12:1—In this letter written to Paul, they had also asked him about spiritual gifts.

1 Corinthians 16:1—This letter also had asked about giving.

TUNE-UP #14

1. Love is meant to be the mark of a Christian.
2. Love is the distinguishing difference between one who knows God and one who does not know God.

Both passages point to the supremacy of love.

TUNE-UP #15

1. The wilderness
2. Luke 4:14–9:50
3. Activities
4. Miracles

TUNE-UP #16

They were located in several cities. Jews assembled at synagogues to pray and hear the law read. In Acts, the early church assembled in these.

TUNE-UP #17

The Jewish synagogue began during the Babylonian exile. Synagogues were used during times when the Jews had no temple.

TUNE-UP #18

1. Northernmost section of Palestine.
2. Covered one-third of Palestine, approximately 2,000 square miles. Approximate population, 2–3 million.
3. Mountains and hills covered by forests. Broad valleys filled with rich agriculture.
4. Influential wealthy Jews. Most worked in fields; however, some had commercial jobs. They were devoted to their religious heritage.

TUNE-UP #19

1. It was through the Holy Spirit, which began at His baptism and sustained Him in the wilderness.
2. At this point in His ministry, He was a popular attraction. Later He was rejected.
3. It contradicted Jewish prejudices.

TUNE-UP #20

1. Words are not enough. One must act on what Christ says.
2. No.
3. It was the conclusion to His Sermon on the Mount. The parable was meant to reinforce the need to act on what He had said.
4. Not only did the house on the rock not fall, it could not be shaken because of its deep foundation in a rock. The house on the sand lacked a lasting foundation.

TUNE-UP #21

Judges 7:12 is hyperbole.
Matthew 5:13 is an allegory.
1 Kings 18:27 is a simile.
Mark 7:19 is irony.
Galatians 2:20 is a paradox.
Genesis 49:9 is a metaphor.
Luke 4:23 is a proverb.
Habakkuk 3:10 is personification.

TUNE-UP #22

1. As the lamb's blood was shed to save the people, so Christ's blood was shed to save us (Exodus 12:12, 13).
2. As the lamb was unblemished, so Christ was our *perfect* sacrifice (Exodus 12:5).
3. As the lamb's bones were not broken, so Christ's were unbroken (Exodus 12:46).

TUNE-UP #23

1. Psalm 69:9—"Zeal for thy house will consume me." This was a messianic pronouncement of David.
   John 2:19—"Destroy this temple, and in three days I will raise it up." This was a messianic pronouncement of Jesus.
2. Psalm 69:9—The fulfillment of this was being shown through the actions of Jesus in cleansing the temple.
   John 2:19—This was literally fulfilled when Christ raised from the dead (Mark 14:58; 15:29; 16:6).

TUNE-UP #24

Proverbs 25:25 is emblematic parallelism.
Psalm 29:1, 2 is stairlike parallelism.

Psalm 103:3 is synonymous parallelism.
Proverbs 14:18 is antithetic parallelism.

TUNE-UP #25

POSSIBLE OBSERVATIONS:
1. God approves of those who interpret the Bible correctly.
2. Diligence is necessary for correct interpretation.
3. Christians are likened to workmen.

INTERPRETATION:
Those who study God's Word are to strive for a correct interpretation, like a diligent worker who "cuts it straight."

APPLICATION:
One goal in my life should be to strive to always accurately interpret the Word.

FOR FURTHER READING

Burrows, Millar. *What Mean These Stones?* New York: Bobbs Merrill, 1960.

Colson, Charles. *Who Speaks For God?* Westchester: Crossway Books, 1985.

Geisler, Norman L., and William E. Nix. *A General Introduction to the Bible.* Chicago: Moody Press, 1968.

Gleason, Archer L. *A Survey of Old Testament Introduction.* Chicago: Moody Press, 1964.

Glueck, Nelson. *Rivers in the Desert: History of Neteg.* Philadelphia: Jewish Publications Society of America, 1969.

Hendriksen, William. *New Testament Commentary on Luke.* Grand Rapids: Baker Book House, 1978.

Jensen, Irving L. *Enjoying Your Bible.* Chicago: Moody Press, 1969.

Kaiser, Walter. *Toward an Exegetical Theology.* Grand Rapids: Baker Book House, 1981.

Kraeling, Emil G. *Rand McNally Bible Atlas.* New York: Rand McNally & Co., 1956.

Lockyer, Herbert. *All the Parables of the Bible.* Grand Rapids: Zondervan Publishing House, 1963.

McDowell, Josh. *Evidence That Demands a Verdict.* San Bernardino: Campus Crusade For Christ, 1972.

Metzger, Bruce M. *The Text of the New Testament.* Oxford: Oxford University Press, 1968.

New American Standard Bible. Nashville: Thomas Nelson Publishers, 1985.

Packer, J. I. *Keep in Step With the Spirit.* Old Tappan: Fleming H. Revell Co., 1984.

Perry, Lloyd M., and Walden Howard. *How to Study the Bible.* Old Tappan: Fleming H. Revell Co., 1957.

Robertson, A. T. *Introduction to the Textual Criticism of the New Testament.* Nashville: Broadman Press, 1925.

Selle, F. F., and Ewald Plass. *Quotations and Illustrations for Sermons.* Saint Louis: Concordia Publishing House, 1951.

Smith, Wilbur M. *Profitable Bible Study.* Boston: W. A. Wilde Company, 1939.

Smith, William. *A Dictionary of the Bible.* Grand Rapids: Zondervan Publishing House, 1948.

Sproul, R. C. *Knowing Scripture.* Downers Grove: InterVarsity Press, 1977.

Swindoll, Charles R. *Growing Strong in the Seasons of Life.* Portland: Multnomah Press, 1983.

Thomas, Robert, ed., *New American Standard Exhaustive Concordance.* Nashville: Holman Press, 1981.

Vine, W. E. *Vine's Expository Dictionary of New Testament*

Words. Old Tappan: Fleming H. Revell, n.d.

Wilkinson, Bruce. *Talk Thru the New Testament.* Nashville: Thomas Nelson Publishers, 1983.

Yohn, Rick. *First Hand Joy.* Colorado Springs: Navpress, 1982.

ADDITIONAL USEFUL TOOLS FOR SERIOUS MECHANICS

Baxter, J. Sidlow. *Explore The Book: Six Volumes In One.* Grand Rapids: Wm. B. Eerdmans Publishing Co., 1968.

Brown, Colin. *New International Dictionary of New Testament Theology,* 3 vols. Grand Rapids: Zondervan Publishing House, 1978.

Douglas, J. D. *New Bible Dictionary.* Grand Rapids: Wm. B. Eerdmans Publishing Co., 1962.

Edersheim, Alfred. *The Life and Times of Jesus the Messiah,* 2 vols. Grand Rapids: Wm. B. Eerdmans Publishing Co., 1972.

Hendrikson, William. *New Testament Commentary,* 9 vols. Grand Rapids: Baker Book House, 1975.

Jamieson, Robert, et al. *Unabridged Bible Commentary,* 3 vols. Grand Rapids: Wm. B. Eerdmans Publishing Co., 1974.

Kaiser, Walter. *Toward an Exegetical Theology.* Grand Rapids: Baker Book House, 1981.

Lewis, Gordon R. *Decide for Yourself.* Downers Grove: Inter-Varsity Press, 1970.

Little, Paul E. *Know What You Believe.* Wheaton: Scripture Press, 1970.

May, Herbert G., ed. *Oxford Bible Atlas.* New York: Oxford University Press, Inc., 1962.

Mears, Henrietta C. *What the Bible Is All About.* Glendale: Regal Press, 1977.

Packer, J. I. *God's Words.* Downers Grove: InterVarsity Press, 1981.

Tenney, Merrill C., ed. *The Zondervan Pictorial Encyclopedia of the Bible,* 5 vols. Grand Rapids: Zondervan Publishing House, 1975.

Thiessen, Henry Clarence. *Lectures in Systematic Theology.* Grand Rapids: Wm. B. Eerdmans Publishing Co., 1949.

Unger, Merrill F. *Unger's Bible Handbook.* Chicago: Moody Press, 1966.

Virkler, Henry A. *Hermeneutics.* Grand Rapids: Baker Book House, 1981.